THE DUCHESS OF MALFI

THE DUCHESS OF MALFI

A Play Written by
JOHN WEBSTER

Edited by

C. VAUGHAN

GYAN

Published by

GYAN

Gyan Publishing House
5, Ansari Road
Daryaganj, New Delhi-110002
Phone: 011-47034999, 9811692060
E-mail: books@gyanbooks.com

Distribution Network
gyanbooks.com
India, USA, Canada, UK, Australia

ISBN: 978-93-6208-137-7 (PB)
First Published, 1614

2nd Impression 2024

Printed at: Gyan Press, Delhi.

THE DUCHESS OF MALFI
Author: JOHN WEBSTER, Editor: C. VAUGHAN

THE TEMPLE DRAMATISTS

Webster's DUCHESS OF MALFI

Malfi. After Turner.

THE DUCHESS OF MALFI

A Play written by

JOHN WEBSTER

Edited with a Preface, Notes and Glossary by

C. VAUGHAN, M.A.

J. M. DENT AND CO.
ALDINE HOUSE : LONDON
1900

PREFACE

Early Editions of the Play. *The Duchess of Malfi* was first printed as a small Quarto, in 1623. It was reprinted, with some trifling variations, in 1640 and 1678. But, according to Dyce, the First Edition is 'by far the most correct of the Quartos.' It has been used, for purposes of collation with Dyce's text, in the preparation of the present volume. No Edition, subsequent to the first three, can claim any authority.

Life and other Works of Webster. In the second generation of Elizabethan dramatists, if the name Elizabethan may be given a wide meaning, there is no figure more marked than Webster's. Of his life we know little, and nothing of importance. His career as dramatist began in the closing years of the Queen's reign, and seems to have lasted through that of her successor.[2] Whether he lived on into the days of Charles I. is quite uncertain.[1]

1 See the question discussed by Dyce. Introduction, pp. xvi-xxix.

2 The following are the Plays, wholly or in part by Webster, of which trace has come down to us:—

The Guise. [See Dedication to *The Devil's Law-Case* and Henslowe's *Diary*, p. 202: Nov. 1601.]

Cæsar's Fall. [Written in partnership with Munday, Drayton, Middleton, etc. Henslowe's *Diary*, p. 221: May 1602.]

The Two Harpes (?) [Written in partnership with Munday, Drayton, Middleton, and Dekker. Henslowe's *Diary*, p. 222: May 1602.]

Lady Jane. [Written in partnership with Chettle, Dekker, Heywood, and Smith; probably part of the first version of what was afterwards (1607) published as *The Famous History of Sir Thomas Wyatt.* Henslowe's *Diary*, p. 242: Oct. 1602.]

But our ignorance of his outer life matters little; it is clear that his whole soul went out in his dramas. Here his range was unusually wide even for an age where width, no less than depth, was the rule. His comedies—written in partnership with Dekker, and, in one instance, with Rowley—are full of life and of that keen observation which came by nature to the contemporaries of Shakespeare. And in one of them—*Westward Ho*—there is a strain of passion and poetry which, however strangely it may contrast with the bald setting that surrounds it, certainly gives it a place among the

---

Christmas Comes but Once a Year. [Written in partnership with Chettle, Dekker, and Heywood. Henslowe's *Diary*, pp. 243-4: Nov. 1602.]

Additions to Marston's *Malcontent.* [See the Title-page of the later Quarto of 1604. The Play must have been very congenial to Webster, and may even have suggested some touches in *The Duchess of Malfi*, particularly as to the character of Bosola. But it is probable that Webster only wrote the *Induction.*]

Westward Ho. [Printed as Quarto in 1607: possibly acted as early as 1605. In partnership with Dekker.]

Northward Ho. [Printed as Quarto in 1607. In partnership with Dekker.]

A Cure for a Cuckold. [Attributed on the Title-page of the Quarto of 1661, the earliest known text, to Webster and Rowley.]

Vittoria Corombona. [Printed in 1612.]

The Duchess of Malfi. [Printed in 1623. See Introduction.]

The Devil's Law-Case. [Printed in 1623.]

A Late Murder of the Son upon the Mother. [Licensed in 1624. In partnership with Ford.]

Appius and Virginia. [Printed in 1654.]

Monuments of Honour. [A City Pageant or Masque, printed in 1624.]

The publisher of *A Cure for a Cuckold* also printed, in the same year, a Play called *The Thracian Wonder*, as 'written by John Webster and William Rowley.' But, so far as Webster is concerned, this seems to rest on a mistake. See Dyce's *Introduction*, p. xv. (Routledge's *Old Dramatists*).

Webster also wrote *A Monumental Column*, a fine Elegy on the death of Prince Henry, 1613.

more memorable pieces of an age rich beyond all others in comic genius.[1]

But no one can doubt that his true field was Tragedy. Even in his lighter vein he seems to have needed tragic material before he could give free play to his extraordinary powers. *The Devil's Law-Case*, his one tragi-comedy, is, save for the closing scene, entirely tragic in plot and conduct. And it shows dramatic powers of a higher kind, a keener sense of effect, and a subtler appreciation of the finer shades of character, than can be found in any of his comedies.

It is, however, in strict Tragedy that Webster is at his greatest. Ever since Lamb wrote in praise of them, *Vittoria Corombona* and *The Duchess of Malfi* have been universally accepted as among the first masterpieces of the Elizabethan drama. They show a closer study of Shakespeare's work than is to be found in any other dramatist of his time; and they show also a nearer approach to his spirit.[2] There is in both plays a blending of tragedy with pathos, of pity with terror, that has never been surpassed, and perhaps not even equalled, except by Shakespeare himself. Besides this, we find in them that depth of reflection, combining profound humanity

[1] *Westward Ho*, Act IV. Sc. ii.

[2] See in particular the scene—clearly inspired by that of Ophelia's madness—where Cornelia lays out the body of Marcello for burial. Routledge's Edition, p. 45. Compare the Introduction to *Vittoria Corombona*:—'Detraction is the sworn friend to ignorance: for mine own part, I have ever cherished my good opinion of other men's worthy labours; especially of that full and heightened style of Master Chapman; the laboured and understanding works of Master Jonson; the no less worthy composures of the both worthily excellent Master Beaumont and Master Fletcher; and lastly (without wrong last to be named) the right happy and copious industry of Master Shakespeare, Master Dekker, and Master Heywood; wishing that what I write may be read by their light.'

with intense imagination, which is the surest mark of a great dramatic poet, and, for that reason, is the highest quality of Shakespeare.

The one point in which Webster falls behind, not Shakespeare alone but certain other of his contemporaries, is humour. That there are scenes, and even characters, truly humorous in his writings, few readers will deny. But their humour is always of the more obvious kind; it is apt to be elaborate and metallic; it is akin, though on a lower level, to the saturnine humour of Jonson; it has nothing of the mellowness, of the sunny sympathy with all sides of life, which is the glory of Cervantes and Shakespeare and, in a less degree, of Dekker. Had Webster possessed this quality, and had he also known the art of dramatic construction—in this he is lamentably deficient—it would hardly have been left to the devotion of Lamb and Hazlitt, well-nigh two centuries after his death, to discover his greatness.

The two Plays above mentioned are unquestionably the finest of Webster's Tragedies. And in some sense they may be described as companion pictures, as studies of good and bad in the character of women. Outside of Shakespeare's plays, there is perhaps no woman at once so noble and so womanly as Webster's ill-fated Duchess.[1] But no less striking, though in a very different way, is the 'White Devil' of *Vittoria Corombona.* She is a supreme example of the splendid sinner, the criminal who fascinates, if she is not redeemed, by the indomitable will; own sister to Lady Macbeth, to Lucrèce Borgia, to Clytemnestra—*γυναικὸς ἀνδρόβουλον ἐλπίζον κέαρ.*

[1] 'Whether the spirit of greatness or of woman
Reign most in her, I know not.' Act I. Sc. i.

Date of the Play. It seems probable that both Plays fall within the same period of Webster's life. For, though *Vittoria* was printed in 1612, and *The Duchess* not till 1623, it is certain that the latter must have been written at least five years earlier than its publication. Burbage, who acted the part of Ferdinand on the original production of the Play, died at the beginning of 1619; and its first performance can therefore hardly be placed later than 1618. If we are right in assuming that *Vittoria* was printed soon after its first production—and that is the natural inference from some words which refer in detail to its cool reception and which are omitted in the second edition [1]—then both Plays will belong to the earlier manhood of Webster's life and to the years immediately following Shakespeare's withdrawal from any active part in the management of the Theatre.[2]

Source of the Play. The story as treated by Webster and other Writers. The plot of *The Duchess of Malfi* was apparently drawn from Painter's *Palace of Pleasure*, a large collection of tales published in the early years of Elizabeth's reign,[3] and Painter, in his turn, drew from Belleforest's French

[1] 'It was acted in *so dull a time of winter, presented in* so open and black a theatre that it wanted . . . a full and understanding auditory.' The words italicised were omitted in the later editions.

[2] See note, p. 146.

[3] Tome I. was published in 1566: Tome II. in 1567. It is the latter which contains *The Duchess of Malfi*. The Collection was re-edited by Mr. Jacobs in 1890: the original of Webster's Drama is to be found in Vol. iii., pp. 3-43, of his edition. Belleforest's *Histoires Tragiques* was published in 1565.

adaptation of the *Novelle* of Bandello.[1] But Webster owed nothing beyond the dry bones of the story to Painter; the living spirit and the characters are entirely his own. Thus the whole endeavour of Painter is to throw our sympathies against Antonio and the Duchess and to prove their misfortunes to be the natural nemesis of their 'notable folly.'[2]

Starting from this unpromising commonplace, he could not but give a very different version of the characters from that which presented itself to the inspired genius of Webster. The Duchess, in the opening of his story, is a wanton widow—a kinswoman, though by several removes, of the Wife of Bath—who 'fantasies in the night'—and at great length—'upon the discourse of her appetites.' It is only on second thoughts that she 'did set her mind on Antonio or fantasy to marry him.' A sordid contrast to the unstudied and stainless purity of Webster's heroine, and to the dignity which, in a position seemingly almost desperate, still remains dignity without an effort. And

[1] There is also a drama—*El Mayordomo de la Duquesa de Amalfi*—by Lope de Vega. It was first printed in 1618, in Vol. XI. of his Collected Works. It is clear that neither Englishman nor Spaniard had seen the other's Play. The only scene in Lope, even distantly recalling Webster's *Duchess*, is that in which the Duchess makes asides of love to Antonio, while professing to dismiss him from her service. The most striking part of the Play is the last Act, in which there is a genuine reconciliation between Antonio and his stepson and an apparent one between him and Julio, brother of the Duchess. Julio then treacherously poisons Antonio and the children, and the Play closes with a burning denunciation from the Duchess. Throughout the Play—as its name indicates—it is on Antonio rather than the Duchess that the interest is centred.

[2] The Argument prefixed to Bandello's Tale will give a fair notion of the treatment adopted by all three 'novelists':—

'Fasi vedere in questa novella il poco avvedimento d'una signora, che per illeciti appetiti abbassandosi del suo grado si conjunge ad infimo di se . . . Si dimostra il folle amore di quanto male sia causa e la poca prudenza d'una donna negli effetti suoi in avilire per i carnali appetiti la sua nobiltà.' —Ed. Milano (1560) t. I. pp. 190-198.

this is but one instance of what runs throughout the version followed by Painter. Of the gracious love between wife and husband, of the constancy which lives unshaken through unimaginable tortures—'I am Duchess of Malfi still'—of the sweet care for her children that leaps to her lips in the very agony of death,—of all this there is no hint in the *Palace of Pleasure*; or, at best, what is so bald as to suggest nothing of what Webster has drawn from it.

The same coarseness of touch is seen in Painter's handling of the other characters. Antonio is little better than a presumptuous upstart. Ferdinand and the Cardinal, the champions of family honour at the beginning of the tale, become vulgar assassins—the Cardinal, in fact, is a sad example of the accomplished villainy that good Protestants may expect to find in Papists—at the close.[1] Lastly, Bosola, certainly one of the most subtle and profound of Webster's creations, is a mere name, a 'bloody beast,' to Painter.

It is the old story. The 'source' of a work of genius commonly counts for little or nothing; and the study of it is only of value for the sake of showing what is *not* in it. 'Je prends mon bien où je le trouve,' said Molière. 'I take it where I do *not* find it,' would be the most accurate translation.

Unity of the Play. On one of the additions made by Webster to his original, some question may arise. The whole

1 'Behold here the noble fact of a Cardinal, and what savour it hath of Christian purity. . . . Is this the sweet observation of the Apostles, of whom they vaunt themselves to be the successors and followers?' etc. Vol. iii. p. 42. It is only fair to say that this is a faithful translation from Belleforest, t. ii. p. 30.

of the last Act is virtually of his own making. Does it, or does it not, interfere with the unity of the piece? For strict purposes of dramatic effect the genius of the Play, to borrow Johnson's phrase, will probably be held to come in and go out with the Duchess. And it may be doubted whether, in his instinctive sense of concentration, Shakespeare would not have ended the drama with her death. Certainly in none of his tragedies is the interest so divided as it is between the last Act and the preceding ones of Webster's *Duchess*. But, on the other hand, who would have missed the ghastly inveteracy of Ferdinand's soul-stricken ravings, or the unequal combat of the Cardinal with avenging nemesis, or the unavailing yet intense remorse of Bosola?

The truth is that, being what he was, Webster could hardly have written otherwise than as he did. His imagination had supped full of horrors; and it was precisely the horrors of an evil conscience, the most tragic of all horrors, that he best loved to portray.[1] The whole drama, like its counterpart *The White Devil*, is charged with an overmastering sense of the depravity of Courts; and this, with the retribution dogging the criminals, is the theme that the last Act relentlessly drives home. In *The White Devil*, loosely as the play is built, this preoccupation with what may fairly be called a moral aim brought with it no sacrifice of dramatic unity; for there the interest is centred throughout upon the criminals. But in *The Duchess* it is not so; and it is hard to see how the end of the

[1] A crucial instance of this may be found in the terrible brevity of Vittoria's dying words—

'My soul like to a ship in a black storm
Is driven, I know not whither.'

dramatist could have been gained at less cost than in fact he paid. The unity of action, no doubt, is lost; but the unity of subject, and to some extent, notably in the case of Bosola, the unity of character, are preserved.

Analogy between *The Duchess of Malfi* and other Plays of Webster. The sombre cast of imagination, the lingering on images of death and corruption, so noticeable in this play, reappears, as is well known, in all Webster's most characteristic work; forcing its way significantly into 'the very temple of delight' where sensual passion is the one thought of the characters set before us by the dramatist. The two most passionate scenes that he created are both mocked by emblems or counterfeits of death; and the haunting shapes that gibber round the 'last presence-chamber' of the Duchess are not more eloquent of his brooding melancholy than the 'filthy hag' who personates the mistress of the Earl in *Westward Ho*, or the yew-tree that frowns on the wanton dream of the White Devil.

On this point Lamb has written as no other critic could have done. His words have often been quoted, but they will bear quoting once again:—'All the several parts of the dreadful apparatus with which the Duchess's death is ushered in are not more remote from the conceptions of ordinary vengeance, than the strange character of suffering which they seem to bring upon their victims is beyond the imagination of ordinary poets. As they are not like inflictions *of this life*, so her language seems *not of this world*. She has lived among horrors till she is become "native and endowed unto that element." She speaks the dialect of despair, her tongue has a snatch of Tartarus and the souls in bale. What are "Luke's iron crown," the brazen bull of Perillus, Procrustes' bed, to the waxen images which counterfeit death, to the wild masque of madmen, the tomb-maker, the bell-man, the living person's dirge, the mortification by degrees! To move a horror skilfully, to touch a *soul* to the quick, to lay upon fear as much as it can bear, to wean and weary a life till it is ready to drop and then step in with mortal instruments to take its last forfeit: this only a Webster can do. Writers of an inferior genius may "upon horror's head horrors accumulate," but they cannot do this. They mistake quantity for quality, they "terrify babes with painted devils," but they know not how a soul is capable of being moved; their terrors want dignity, their affrightments are without decorum.'

Webster's place in the Development of the Elizabethan Drama. This habit of dallying with thoughts of death, and his unapproached command of all the symbolism of mortality, caused a great critic of our own day to describe Webster's genius as 'macabre.' The word, it may well be thought, does Webster something less than justice. It implies a love of the grotesque, which is hardly to be found in him; and it suggests a trickery and set purpose of ghastliness which is altogether alien to the noble simplicity of his nature. But if no more be meant than that his conceptions and his imagery alike are sombre, then an obvious truth is expressed; and a truth which serves to illustrate Webster's place in the development—some would frankly say the decadence—of the English Drama and his relation to some among the most famous of his contemporaries.

As we turn to Webster, we feel at once that the joyousness, which is the clearest note of Marlowe and other writers of the earlier generation, has for ever passed away. The pride of life, the readiness to follow passion wherever it may lead, which inspires every line of *Tamburlaine* or of *Romeo and Juliet*, has yielded to the spirit of weighing and questioning—we may almost say, to a sense of hollowness in things—such as meets us in *Hamlet* or in *Lear*. In Webster, indeed, the gloom is far deeper and more settled than was possible to the well-poised and essentially buoyant soul of Shakespeare. It can hardly be denied that there is something morbid in his cast of thought. And, though morbidness is not in itself decadence, we feel that, where the one is, the other can seldom be far off.

And that is the prevailing sense that we carry away from the Plays of Webster. Neither he nor Ford, who in many ways is like-minded with him, could have written except when dissolution was at work around them. They themselves remain untainted; and the elements of decay which we seem to recognise in their work are transformed into fresh shapes of living beauty by the potent fire of their genius. Their work is more closely knit, both in thought and style, than that of Fletcher; they are free from the straining for effect that we find even in the noblest work of Massinger.[1] They are thus touched by neither of the two dissolving forces which can be traced both in earlier and later samples of the drama of their time. But the line that parts them from Massinger is slightly drawn. It is in the use of their materials, rather than in the nature of them, that the difference must be found. They live in the age of decadence, but they are not of it. And this is perhaps still more true of Webster than it is of Ford.

1 See his *Duke of Milan*—a Play on the same theme as *Othello*; but the difference of treatment is significant.

DUCHESS OF MALFI

DRAMATIS PERSONÆ

FERDINAND, Duke of Calabria
CARDINAL, his brother
ANTONIO BOLOGNA, Steward of the Household to the Duchess
DELIO, his friend
DANIEL DE BOSOLA, Gentleman of the Horse to the Duchess
CASTRUCCIO
MARQUIS OF PESCARA
COUNT MALATESTI
RODERIGO
SILVIO
GRISOLAN
DOCTOR
The Several Madmen

DUCHESS OF MALFI
CARIOLA, her woman
JULIA, Castruccio's wife, and the Cardinal's mistress
Old Lady

Ladies, Children, Pilgrims, Executioners, Officers, and Attendants.

THE DUCHESS OF MALFI

ACT I

SCENE I

Malfi. The presence-chamber in the palace of the Duchess.

Enter Antonio and Delio.

Delio. You are welcome to your country, dear Antonio;
You have been long in France, and you return
A very formal Frenchman in your habit:
How do you like the French court?
Ant. I admire it:
In seeking to reduce both state and people
To a fix'd order, their judicious king
Begins at home; quits first his royal palace
Of flattering sycophants, of dissolute
And infamous persons,—which he sweetly terms
His master's master-piece, the work of heaven;
Considering duly that a prince's court
Is like a common fountain, whence should flow

Pure silver drops in general, but if 't chance
Some curs'd example poison 't near the head,
Death and diseases through the whole land spread.
And what is 't makes this blessèd government
But a most provident council, who dare freely
Inform him the corruption of the times?
Though some o' the court hold it presumption
To instruct princes what they ought to do,
It is a noble duty to inform them
What they ought to foresee.—Here comes Bosola,
The only court-gall; yet I observe his railing
Is not for simple love of piety:
Indeed, he rails at those things which he wants;
Would be as lecherous, covetous, or proud,
Bloody, or envious, as any man,
If he had means to be so.—Here 's the cardinal.

Enter Cardinal and Bosola.

Bos. I do haunt you still.
Card. So.
Bos. I have done you better service than to be slighted thus. Miserable age, where only the reward of doing well is the doing of it!
Card. You enforce your merit too much.
Bos. I fell into the galleys in your service; where, for two years together, I wore two towels instead of a shirt, with a knot on the shoulder, after the fashion

of a Roman mantle. Slighted thus! I will thrive some way: black-birds fatten best in hard weather; why not I in these dog-days?

Card. Would you could become honest!

Bos. With all your divinity do but direct me the way to it. I have known many travel far for it, and yet return as arrant knaves as they went forth, because they carried themselves always along with them. [*Exit Cardinal.*] Are you gone? Some fellows, they say, are possessed with the devil, but this great fellow were able to possess the greatest devil, and make him worse.

Ant. He hath denied thee some suit!

Bos. He and his brother are like plum-trees that grow crooked over standing-pools; they are rich and o'er-laden with fruit, but none but crows, pies, and caterpillars feed on them. Could I be one of their flattering panders, I would hang on their ears like a horseleech, till I were full, and then drop off. I pray, leave me. Who would rely upon these miserable dependencies, in expectation to be advanced to-morrow? what creature ever fed worse than hoping Tantalus? nor ever died any man more fearfully than he that hoped for a pardon. There are rewards for hawks and dogs when they have done us service; but for a soldier that hazards his limbs in a battle, nothing but a kind of geometry is his last supportation.

Delio. Geometry!

Bos. Ay, to hang in a fair pair of slings, take his latter swing in the world upon an honourable pair of crutches, from hospital to hospital. Fare ye well, sir: and yet do not you scorn us; for places in the court are but like beds in the hospital, where this man's head lies at that man's foot, and so lower and lower. [*Exit.*

Del. I knew this fellow seven years in the galleys
For a notorious murder; and 'twas thought
The cardinal suborn'd it: he was releas'd
By the French general, Gaston de Foix,
When he recover'd Naples.

Ant. 'Tis great pity
He should be thus neglected: I have heard
He's very valiant. This foul melancholy
Will poison all his goodness; for, I'll tell you,
If too immoderate sleep be truly said
To be an inward rust unto the soul,
It then doth follow want of action
Breeds all black malcontents; and their close rearing,
Like moths in cloth, do hurt for want of wearing.

Delio. The presence 'gins to fill: you promis'd me
To make me the partaker of the natures
Of some of your great courtiers.

Ant. The lord cardinal's
And other strangers' that are now in court?
I shall.—Here comes the great Calabrian duke.

Enter Ferdinand, Castruccio, Silvio, Roderigo, Grisolan, and Attendants.

Ferd. Who took the ring oftenest?

Sil. Antonio Bologna, my lord.

Ferd. Our sister duchess' great-master of her household? give him the jewel.—When shall we leave this sportive action, and fall to action indeed?

Cast. Methinks, my lord, you should not desire to go to war in person.

Ferd. Now for some gravity:—why, my lord?

Cast. It is fitting a soldier arise to be a prince, but not necessary a prince descend to be a captain.

Ferd. No.

Cast. No, my lord; he were far better do it by a deputy.

Ferd. Why should he not as well sleep or eat by a deputy? this might take idle, offensive, and base office from him, whereas the other deprives him of honour.

Cast. Believe my experience, that realm is never long in quiet where the ruler is a soldier.

Ferd. Thou toldest me thy wife could not endure fighting.

Cast. True, my lord.

Ferd. And of a jest she broke of a captain she met full of wounds: I have forgot it.

Cast. She told him, my lord, he was a pitiful fellow, to lie, like the children of Ismael, all in tents.

Ferd. Why, there's a wit were able to undo all the

chirurgeons o' the city; for although gallants should quarrel, and had drawn their weapons, and were ready to go to it, yet her persuasions would make them put up.

Cast. That she would, my lord.—How do you like my Spanish gennet?

Rod. He is all fire.

Ferd. I am of Pliny's opinion, I think he was begot by the wind; he runs as if he were ballassed with quicksilver.

Sil. True, my lord, he reels from the tilt often.

Rod. Gris. Ha, ha, ha!

Ferd. Why do you laugh? methinks you that are courtiers should be my touch-wood, take fire when I give fire; that is, laugh [but] when I laugh, were the subject never so witty.

Cast. True, my lord: I myself have heard a very good jest, and have scorned to seem to have so silly a wit as to understand it.

Ferd. But I can laugh at your fool, my lord.

Cast. He cannot speak, you know, but he makes faces: my lady cannot abide him.

Ferd. No?

Cast. Nor endure to be in merry company; for she says too much laughing, and too much company, fills her too full of the wrinkle.

Ferd. I would, then, have a mathematical instrument made for herface, that she might not laugh out of compass.—I shall shortly visit you at Milan, Lord Silvio.

Sil. Your grace shall arrive most welcome.

Ferd. You are a good horseman, Antonio: you have excellent riders in France: what do you think of good horsemanship?

Ant. Nobly, my lord: as out of the Grecian horse issued many famous princes, so out of brave horsemanship arise the first sparks of growing resolution, that raise the mind to noble action.

Ferd. You have bespoke it worthily.

Sil. Your brother, the lord cardinal, and sister duchess.

Re-enter Cardinal, with Duchess, Cariola, and Julia.

Card. Are the galleys come about?

Gris. They are, my lord.

Ferd. Here's the Lord Silvio is come to take his leave.

Delio. Now, sir, your promise: what's that cardinal?
I mean his temper? they say he's a brave fellow,
Will play his five thousand crowns at tennis, dance,
Court ladies, and one that hath fought single combats.

Ant. Some such flashes superficially hang on him for form; but observe his inward character: he is a melancholy churchman; the spring in his face is nothing but the engendering of toads; where he is jealous of any man, he lays worse plots for them than ever was imposed on Hercules, for he strews in his way flatterers, panders, intelligencers, atheists, and a thousand such political monsters. He should have been Pope; but instead of coming to it by the primitive decency of the church, he did bestow bribes so largely and so impudently as if he would have carried it away without heaven's knowledge. Some good he hath done——

Delio. You have given too much of him. What's his brother?

Ant. The duke there? a most perverse and turbulent nature:
What appears in him mirth is merely outside;
If he laught heartily, it is to laugh
All honesty out of fashion.

Delio. Twins?

Ant. In quality.
He speaks with others' tongues, and hears men's suits
With others' ears; will seem to sleep o' the bench
Only to entrap offenders in their answers;
Dooms men to death by information;
Rewards by hearsay.

Delio. Then the law to him
Is like a foul, black cobweb to a spider,—
He makes it his dwelling and a prison
To entangle those shall feed him.

Ant. Most true:
He never pays debts unless they be shrewd turns,
And those he will confess that he doth owe.
Last, for his brother there, the cardinal,
They that do flatter him most say oracles

Hang at his lips; and verily I believe them,
For the devil speaks in them.
But for their sister, the right noble duchess,
You never fix'd your eye on three fair medals
Cast in one figure, of so different temper.
For her discourse, it is so full of rapture,
You only will begin then to be sorry
When she doth end her speech, and wish, in wonder,
She held it less vain-glory to talk much,
Than your penance to hear her: whilst she speaks,
She throws upon a man so sweet a look,
That it were able to raise one to a galliard
That lay in a dead palsy, and to dote
On that sweet countenance; but in that look
There speaketh so divine a continence
As cuts off all lascivious and vain hope.
Her days are practis'd in such noble virtue,
That sure her nights, nay, more, her very sleeps,
Are more in heaven than other ladies' shrifts.
Let all sweet ladies break their flattering glasses,
And dress themselves in her.

Delio. Fie, Antonio,
You play the wire-drawer with her commendations.

Ant. I'll case the picture up: only thus much;
All her particular worth grows to this sum,—
She stains the time past, lights the time to come.

Cari. You must attend my lady in the gallery,
Some half an hour hence.

Ant. I shall. [*Exeunt Antonio and Delio.*

Ferd. Sister, I have a suit to you.

Duch. To me, sir?

Ferd. A gentleman here, Daniel de Bosola,
One that was in the galleys——

Duch. Yes, I know him.

Ferd. A worthy fellow he is: pray, let me entreat for
The provisorship of your horse.

Duch. Your knowledge of him
Commends him and prefers him.

Ferd. Call him hither. [*Exit Attendant.*
We [are] now upon parting. Good Lord Silvio,
Do us commend to all our noble friends
At the leaguer.

Sil. Sir, I shall.

Ferd. You are for Milan?

Sil. I am.

Duch. Bring the caroches.—We'll bring you down to the haven.

[*Exeunt Duchess, Silvio, Castruccio, Roderigo, Grisolan, Cariola, Julia, and Attendants.*

Card. Be sure you entertain that Bosola
For your intelligence: I would not be seen in 't;
And therefore many times I have slighted him
When he did court our furtherance, as this morning.

Ferd. Antonio, the great-master of her household,
Had been far fitter.

Card. You are deceiv'd in him

His nature is too honest for such business.—
He comes: I'll leave you. [*Exit.*

Re-enter Bosola.

Bos. I was lur'd to you.
Ferd. My brother, here, the cardinal could never
Abide you.
Bos. Never since he was in my debt.
Ferd. May be some oblique character in your face
Made him suspect you.
Bos. Doth he study physiognomy?
There's no more credit to be given to the face
Than to a sick man's urine, which some call
The physician's whore because she cozens him.
He did suspect me wrongfully.
Ferd. For that
You must give great men leave to take their times.
Distrust doth cause us seldom be deceiv'd:
You see the oft shaking of the cedar-tree
Fastens it more at root.
Bos. Yet, take heed;
For to suspect a friend unworthily
Instructs him the next way to suspect you,
And prompts him to deceive you.
Ferd. There's gold.
Bos. So:
What follows? never rained such showers as these

Without thunderbolts i' the tail of them: whose throat must I cut?

Ferd. Your inclination to shed blood rides post
Before my occasion to use you. I give you that
To live i' the court here, and observe the duchess;
To note all the particulars of her haviour,
What suitors do solicit her for marriage,
And whom she best affects. She's a young widow:
I would not have her marry again.

Bos. No, sir?

Ferd. Do not you ask the reason; but be satisfied.
I say I would not.

Bos. It seems you would create me
One of your familiars.

Ferd. Familiar! what's that?

Bos. Why, a very quaint invisible devil in flesh,—
An intelligencer.

Ferd. Such a kind of thriving thing
I would wish thee; and ere long thou mayst arrive
At a higher place by 't.

Bos. Take your devils,
Which hell calls angels: these curs'd gifts would make
You a corrupter, me an impudent traitor:
And should I take these, they 'd take me [to] hell.

Ferd. Sir, I'll take nothing from you that I have given:
There is a place that I procured for you

This morning, the provisorship o' the horse;
Have you heard on 't?

Bos. No.

Ferd. 'Tis yours: is 't not worth thanks?

Bos. I would have you curse yourself now, that your bounty
(Which makes men truly noble) e'er should make me
A villain. O, that to avoid ingratitude
For the good deed you have done me, I must do
All the ill man can invent! Thus the devil
Candies all sins o'er; and what heaven terms vile,
That names he complimental.

Ferd. Be yourself;
Keep your old garb of melancholy; 'twill express
You envy those that stand above your reach,
Yet strive not to come near 'em: this will gain
Access to private lodgings, where yourself
May, like a politic dormouse——

Bos. As I have seen some
Feed in a lord's dish, half asleep, not seeming
To listen to any talk; and yet these rogues
Have cut his throat in a dream. What 's my place?
The provisorship o' the horse? say, then, my corruption
Grew out of horse-dung: I am your creature.

Ferd. Away!

Bos. Let good men, for good deeds, covet good fame,
Since place and riches oft are bribes of shame:
Sometimes the devil doth preach. [*Exit.*

Re-enter Duchess, Cardinal, and Cariola.

Card. We are to part from you; and your own discretion
Must now be your director.
Ferd. You are a widow:
You know already what man is; and therefore
Let not youth, high promotion, eloquence——
Card. No,
Nor anything without the addition, honour,
Sway your high blood.
Ferd. Marry! they are most luxurious
Will wed twice.
Card. O, fie!
Ferd. Their livers are more spotted
Than Laban's sheep.
Duch. Diamonds are of most value,
They say, that have pass'd through most jewellers' hands.
Ferd. Whores by that rule are precious.
Duch. Will you hear me?
I'll never marry.
Card. So most widows say;
But commonly that motion lasts no longer
Than the turning of an hour-glass: the funeral sermon
And it end both together.
Ferd. Now hear me:

You live in a rank pasture, here, i' the court;
There is a kind of honey-dew that 's deadly;
'Twill poison your fame; look to 't: be not cunning;
For they whose faces do belie their hearts
Are witches ere they arrive at twenty years,
Ay, and give the devil suck.

Duch. This is terrible good counsel.

Ferd. Hypocrisy is woven of a fine small thread,
Subtler than Vulcan's engine: yet, believe 't,
Your darkest actions, nay, your privat'st thoughts,
Will come to light.

Card. You may flatter yourself,
And take your own choice; privately be married
Under the eaves of night——

Ferd. Think 't the best voyage
That e'er you made; like the irregular crab,
Which, though 't goes backward, thinks that it goes right
Because it goes its own way: but observe,
Such weddings may more properly be said
To be executed than celebrated.

Card. The marriage night
Is the entrance into some prison.

Ferd. And those joys,
Those lustful pleasures, are like heavy sleeps
Which do fore-run man's mischief.

Card. Fare you well.
Wisdom begins at the end: remember it. [*Exit.*

Duch. I think this speech between you both was studied,
It came so roundly off.
Ferd. You are my sister;
This was my father's poniard, do you see?
I 'd be loth to see 't look rusty, 'cause 'twas his.
I would have you give o'er these chargeable revels:
A visor and a mask are whispering-rooms
That were never built for goodness;—fare ye well;—
And women like that part which, like the lamprey,
Hath never a bone in 't.
Duch. Fie, sir!
Ferd. Nay,
I mean the tongue; variety of courtship:
What cannot a neat knave with a smooth tale
Make a woman believe? Farewell, lusty widow.
[*Exit.*
Duch. Shall this move me? If all my royal kindred
Lay in my way unto this marriage,
I 'd make them my low footsteps: and even now,
Even in this hate, as men in some great battles,
By apprehending danger, have achiev'd
Almost impossible actions (I have heard soldiers say so),
So I through frights and threatenings will assay
This dangerous venture. Let old wives report
I wink'd and chose a husband.—Cariola,
To thy known secrecy I have given up
More than my life,—my fame.

Cari. Both shall be safe;
For I'll conceal this secret from the world
As warily as those that trade in poison
Keep poison from their children.
Duch. Thy protestation
Is ingenious and hearty: I believe it.
Is Antonio come?
Cari. He attends you.
Duch. Good dear soul,
Leave me; but place thyself behind the arras,
Where thou mayst overhear us. Wish me good speed;
For I am going into a wilderness,
Where I shall find nor path nor friendly clew
To be my guide.
[*Cariola goes behind the arras.*

Enter Antonio.

I sent for you: sit down;
Take pen and ink, and write: are you ready?
Ant. Yes.
Duch. What did I say?
Ant. That I should write somewhat.
Duch. O, I remember.
After these triumphs and this large expense
It's fit, like thrifty husbands, we inquire
What's laid up for to-morrow.
Ant. So please your beauteous excellence.

Duch. Beauteous!
Indeed, I thank you: I look young for your sake;
You have ta'en my cares upon you.
Ant. I'll fetch your grace
The particulars of your revenue and expense.
Duch. O, you are
An upright treasurer: but you mistook;
For when I said I meant to make inquiry
What's laid up for to-morrow, I did mean
What's laid up yonder for me.
Ant. Where?
Duch. In heaven.
I am making my will (as 'tis fit princes should,
In perfect memory), and, I pray, sir, tell me,
Were not one better make it smiling, thus,
Than in deep groans and terrible ghastly looks,
As if the gifts we parted with procur'd
That violent distraction?
Ant. O, much better.
Duch. If I had a husband now, this care were quit:
But I intend to make you overseer.
What good deed shall we first remember? say.
Ant. Begin with that first good deed began i' the world
After man's creation, the sacrament of marriage:
I'd have you first provide for a good husband;
Give him all.
Duch. All!
Ant. Yes, your excellent self.

Duch. In a winding-sheet?
Ant. In a couple.
Duch. Saint Winifred, that were a strange will!
Ant. 'Twere stranger if there were no will in you
To marry again.
Duch. What do you think of marriage?
Ant. I take 't, as those that deny purgatory,
It locally contains or heaven or hell;
There's no third place in 't.
Duch. How do you affect it?
Ant. My banishment, feeding my melancholy,
Would often reason thus.
Duch. Pray, let's hear it.
Ant. Say a man never marry, nor have children,
What takes that from him? only the bare name
Of being a father, or the weak delight
To see the little wanton ride a-cock-horse
Upon a painted stick, or hear him chatter
Like a taught starling.
Duch. Fie, fie, what's all this?
One of your eyes is blood-shot; use my ring to'
They say 'tis very sovereign: 'twas my wedding-ring,
And I did vow never to part with it
But to my second husband.
Ant. You have parted with it now.
Duch. Yes, to help your eye-sight.
Ant. You have made me stark blind.

Duch. How?
Ant. There is a saucy and ambitious devil
Is dancing in this circle.
Duch. Remove him.
Ant. How?
Duch. There needs small conjuration, when your finger
May do it: thus; is it fit?
[*She puts the ring upon his finger: he kneels.*
Ant. What said you?
Duch. Sir,
This goodly roof of yours is too low built;
I cannot stand upright in 't nor discourse,
Without I raise it higher: raise yourself;
Or, if you please, my hand to help you: so.
[*Raises him.*
Ant. Ambition, madam, is a great man's madness,
That is not kept in chains and close-pent rooms,
But in fair lightsome lodgings, and is girt
With the wild noise of prattling visitants,
Which makes it lunatic beyond all cure.
Conceive not I am so stupid but I aim
Whereto your favours tend: but he's a fool
That, being a-cold, would thrust his hands i' the fire
To warm them.
Duch. So, now the ground's broke,
You may discover what a wealthy mine
I make you lord of.
Ant. O my unworthiness!

Duch. You were ill to sell yourself:
This darkening of your worth is not like that
Which tradesmen use i' the city; their false lights
Are to rid bad wares off: and I must tell you,
If you will know where breathes a cómplete man
(I speak it without flattery), turn your eyes,
And progress through yourself.
Ant. Were there nor heaven nor hell,
I should be honest: I have long serv'd virtue,
And ne'er ta'en wages of her.
Duch. Now she pays it.
The misery of us that are born great!
We are forc'd to woo, because none dare woo us;
And as a tyrant doubles with his words,
And fearfully equivocates, so we
Are forc'd to express our violent passions
In riddles and in dreams, and leave the path
Of simple virtue, which was never made
To seem the thing it is not. Go, go brag
You have left me heartless; mine is in your bosom:
I hope 'twill multiply love there. You do tremble:
Make not your heart so dead a piece of flesh,
To fear more than to love me. Sir, be confident:
What is't distracts you? This is flesh and blood, sir;
'Tis not the figure cut in alabaster
Kneels at my husband's tomb. Awake, awake, man!
I do here put off all vain ceremony,
And only do appear to you a young widow

That claims you for her husband, and, like a widow,
I use but half a blush in 't.
Ant. Truth speak for me;
I will remain the constant sanctuary
Of your good name.
Duch. I thank you, gentle love:
And 'cause you shall not come to me in debt,
Being now my steward, here upon your lips
I sign your *Quietus est.* This you should have begg'd now:
I have seen children oft eat sweetmeats thus,
As fearful to devour them too soon.
Ant. But for your brothers?
Duch. Do not think of them:
All discord without this circumference
Is only to be pitied, and not fear'd:
Yet, should they know it, time will easily
Scatter the tempest.
Ant. These words should be mine,
And all the parts you have spoke, if some part of it
Would not have savour'd flattery.
Duch. Kneel.
[*Cariola comes from behind the arras.*
Ant. Ha!
Duch. Be not amaz'd; this woman 's of my counsel:
I have heard lawyers say, a contract in a chamber
Per verba presenti is absolute marriage.
[*She and Antonio kneel.*

Bless, heaven, this sacred gordian, which let violence
Never untwine!
Ant. And may our sweet affections, like the spheres,
Be still in motion!
Duch. Quickening, and make
The like soft music!
Ant. That we may imitate the loving palms,
Best emblem of a peaceful marriage,
That never bore fruit, divided!
Duch. What can the church force more?
Ant. That fortune may not know an accident,
Either of joy or sorrow, to divide
Our fixèd wishes!
Duch. How can the church build faster?
We now are man and wife, and 'tis the church
That must but echo this.—Maid, stand apart:
I now am blind.
Ant. What's your conceit in this?
Duch. I would have you lead your fortune by the hand
Unto your marriage-bed:
(You speak in me this, for we now are one:)
We'll only lie, and talk together, and plot
To appease my humorous kindred; and if you please,
Like the old tale in Alexander and Lodowick,
Lay a naked sword between us, keep us chaste.

O, let me shrowd my blushes in your bosom,
Since 'tis the treasury of all my secrets!
[*Exeunt Duchess and Antonio.*

Cari. Whether the spirit of greatness or of woman
Reign most in her, I know not; but it shows
A fearful madness: I owe her much of pity. [*Exit.*

ACT II

SCENE I

Malfi. An apartment in the palace of the Duchess.

Enter Bosola and Castruccio.

Bos. You say you would fain be taken for an eminent courtier?

Cast. 'Tis the very main of my ambition.

Bos. Let me see: you have a reasonable good face for't already, and your night-cap expresses your ears sufficient largely. I would have you learn to twirl the strings of your band with a good grace, and in a set speech, at the end of every sentence, to hum three or four times, or blow your nose till it smart again, to recover your memory. When you come to be a president in criminal causes, if you smile upon a prisoner, hang him; but if you frown upon him and threaten him, let him be sure to 'scape the gallows. 13

Cast. I would be a very merry president.

Bos. Do not sup o' nights; 'twill beget you an admirable wit.

Cast. Rather it would make me have a good stomach to quarrel; for they say, your roaring boys eat meat seldom, and that makes them so valiant. But how shall I know whether the people take me for an eminent fellow?

Bos. I will teach a trick to know it: give out you lie a-dying, and if you hear the common people curse you, be sure you are taken for one of the prime night-caps.

Enter an Old Lady.

You come from painting now.

Old Lady. From what?

Bos. Why, from your scurvy face-physic. To behold thee not painted inclines somewhat near a miracle: these in thy face here were deep ruts and foul sloughs the last progress. There was a lady in France that, having had the small-pox, flayed the skin off her face to make it more level; and whereas before she looked like a nutmeg-grater, after she resembled an abortive hedge-hog.

Old Lady. Do you call this painting?

Bos. No, no, but you call [it] careening of an old morphewed lady, to make her disembogue again: there 's rough-cast phrase to your plastic.

Old Lady. It seems you are well acquainted with my closet.

Bos. One would suspect it for a shop of witchcraft, to

find in it the fat of serpents, spawn of snakes, Jews' spittle, and their young children's ordure; and all these for the face. I would sooner eat a dead pigeon taken from the soles of the feet of one sick of the plague, than kiss one of you fasting. Here are two of you, whose sin of your youth is the very patrimony of the physician; makes him renew his foot-cloth with the spring, and change his high-priced courtezan with the fall of the leaf. I do wonder you do not loathe yourselves. Observe my meditation now.

What thing is in this outward form of man
To be belov'd? We account it ominous,
If nature do produce a colt, or lamb,
A fawn, or goat, in any limb resembling
A man, and fly from 't as a prodigy:
Man stands amaz'd to see his deformity
In any other creature but himself.
But in our own flesh though we bear diseases
Which have their true names only ta'en from beasts,—
As the most ulcerous wolf and swinish measle,—
Though we are eaten up of lice and worms,
And though continually we bear about us
A rotten and dead body, we delight
To hide it in rich tissue: all our fear,
Nay, all our terror, is, lest our physician
Should put us in the ground to be made sweet.—

Your wife 's gone to Rome: you two couple, and get you to the wells at Lucca to recover your aches. I have other work on foot.

[*Exeunt Castruccio and Old Lady.*

I observe our duchess
Is sick a-days, she pukes, her stomach seethes,
The fins of her eye-lids look most teeming blue,
She wanes i' the cheek, and waxes fat i' the flank,
And, contrary to our Italian fashion,
Wears a loose-bodied gown: there 's somewhat in't.
I have a trick may chance discover it,
A pretty one; I have bought some apricocks,
The first our spring yields.

Enter Antonio and Delio, talking together apart.

Delio. And so long since married?
You amaze me.

Ant. Let me seal your lips for ever:
For, did I think that anything but the air
Could carry these words from you, I should wish
You had no breath at all.—Now, sir, in your contemplation?
You are studying to become a great wise fellow.

Bos. O, sir, the opinion of wisdom is a foul tetter that runs all over a man's body: if simplicity direct us to have no evil, it directs us to a happy being; for the subtlest folly proceeds from the subtlest wisdom: let me be simply honest.

Ant. I do understand your inside.

Bos. Do you so?

Ant. Because you would not seem to appear to the world
Puff'd up with your preferment, you continue
This out-of-fashion melancholy: leave it, leave it.

Bos. Give me leave to be honest in any phrase, in any compliment whatsoever. Shall I confess myself to you? I look no higher than I can reach: they are the gods that must ride on winged horses. A lawyer's mule of a slow pace will both suit my disposition and business; for, mark me, when a man's mind rides faster than his horse can gallop, they quickly both tire.

Ant. You would look up to heaven, but I think
The devil, that rules i' the air, stands in your light.

Bos. O, sir, you are lord of the ascendant, chief man with the duchess: a duke was your cousin-german removed. Say you were lineally descended from King Pepin, or he himself, what of this? search the heads of the greatest rivers in the world, you shall find them but bubbles of water. Some would think the souls of princes were brought forth by some more weighty cause than those of meaner persons: they are deceived, there 's the same hand to them; the like passions sway them; the same reason that makes a vicar to go to law for a tithe-pig, and undo his neighbours, makes them spoil a whole province, and batter down goodly cities with the cannon.

Enter Duchess and Ladies.

Duch. Your arm, Antonio: do I not grow fat?
I am exceeding short-winded.—Bosola,
I would have you, sir, provide for me a litter;
Such a one as the Duchess of Florence rode in.
Bos. The duchess us'd one when she was great with child.
Duch. I think she did.—Come hither, mend my ruff:
Here, when? thou art such a tedious lady; and
Thy breath smells of lemon-pills: would thou hadst done!
Shall I swoon under thy fingers? I am
So troubled with the mother!
Bos. [*aside.*] I fear too much.
Duch. I have heard you say that the French courtiers
Wear their hats on 'fore the king.
Ant. I have seen it.
Duch. In the presence?
Ant. Yes.
Duch. Why should not we bring up that fashion?
'Tis ceremony more than duty that consists
In the removing of a piece of felt:
Be you the example to the rest o' the court;
Put on your hat first.
Ant. You must pardon me:
I have seen, in colder countries than in France,

Nobles stand bare to the prince; and the distinction
Methought show'd reverently.

Bos. I have a present for your grace.

Duch. For me, sir?

Bos. Apricocks, madam.

Duch. O, sir, where are they?
I have heard of none to-year.

Bos. [*aside.*] Good; her colour rises.

Duch. Indeed, I thank you: they are wondrous fair ones.
What an unskilful fellow is our gardener!
We shall have none this month.

Bos. Will not your grace pare them?

Duch. No: they taste of musk, methinks; indeed they do.

Bos. I know not: yet I wish your grace had par'd 'em.

Duch. Why?

Bos. I forget to tell you, the knave gardener,
Only to raise his profit by them the sooner,
Did ripen them in horse-dung.

Duch. O, you jest.—
You shall judge: pray, taste one.

Ant. Indeed, madam,
I do not love the fruit.

Duch. Sir, you are loth
To rob us of our dainties: 'tis a delicate fruit;
They say they are restorative.

Bos. 'Tis a pretty art,
This grafting.

Duch. 'Tis so; bettering of nature.
Bos. To make a pippin grow upon a crab,
A damson on a black-thorn.—[*Aside.*] How greedily she eats them!
A whirlwind strike off these bawd farthingales!
For, but for that and the loose-bodied gown,
I should have discover'd apparently
The young springal cutting a caper in her belly.
Duch. I thank you, Bosola: they were right good ones,
If they do not make me sick.
Ant. How now, madam!
Duch. This green fruit and my stomach are not friends:
How they swell me!
Bos. [*aside.*] Nay, you are too much swell'd already.
Duch. O, I am in an extreme cold sweat!
Bos. I am very sorry.
Duch. Lights to my chamber!—O good Antonio,
I fear I am undone!
Delio. Lights there, lights!

[*Exeunt Duchess and Ladies.—Exit, on the other side, Bosola.*

Ant. O my most trusty Delio, we are lost!
I fear she's fall'n in labour; and there's left
No time for her remove.
Delio. Have you prepar'd
Those ladies to attend her? and procur'd
That politic safe conveyance for the midwife
Your duchess plotted?

Ant. I have.

Delio. Make use, then, of this forc'd occasion:
Give out that Bosola hath poison'd her
With these apricocks; that will give some colour
For her keeping close.

Ant. Fie, fie, the physicians
Will then flock to her.

Delio. For that you may pretend
She'll use some prepar'd antidote of her own,
Lest the physicians should re-poison her.

Ant. I am lost in amazement: I know not what to think on't. [*Exeunt.*

SCENE II

A hall in the same palace.

Enter Bosola.

Bos. So, so, there's no question but her techiness and most vulturous eating of the apricocks are apparent signs of breeding.

Enter an Old Lady.

Now?

Old Lady. I am in haste, sir.

Bos. There was a young waiting-woman had a monstrous desire to see the glass-house——

Old Lady. Nay, pray, let me go.

Bos. And it was only to know what strange instrument it was should swell up a glass to the fashion of a woman's belly.

Old Lady. I will hear no more of the glass-house. You are still abusing women?

Bos. Who, I? no; only, by the way now and then, mention your frailties. The orange-tree bears ripe and green fruit and blossoms all together; and some of you give entertainment for pure love, but more for more precious reward. The lusty spring smells well; but drooping autumn tastes well. If we have the same golden showers that rained in the time of Jupiter the thunderer, you have the same Danäes still, to hold up their laps to receive them. Didst thou never study the mathematics? 23

Old Lady. What's that, sir?

Bos. Why, to know the trick how to make a many lines meet in one centre. Go, go, give your foster-daughters good counsel: tell them, that the devil takes delight to hang at a woman's girdle, like a false rusty watch, that she cannot discern how the time passes. [*Exit Old Lady.*

Enter Antonio, Roderigo, and Grisolan.

Ant. Shut up the court-gates. 31

Rod. Why, sir? what's the danger?

Ant. Shut up the posterns presently, and call
All the officers o' the court.

Gris. I shall instantly. [*Exit.*

Ant. Who keeps the key o' the park-gate?

Rod. Forobosco.

Ant. Let him bring 't presently.

Re-enter Grisolan with Servants.

First Serv. O, gentleman o' the court, the foulest treason!

Bos. [*aside.*] If that these apricocks should be poison'd now,
Without my knowledge?

First Serv. There was taken even now a Switzer in the duchess' bed-chamber——

Second Serv. A Switzer!

First Serv. With a pistol in his great cod-piece.

Bos. Ha, ha, ha!

First Serv. The cod-piece was the case for 't.

Second Serv. There was a cunning traitor: who would have searched his cod-piece?

First Serv. True, if he had kept out of the ladies' chambers: and all the moulds of his buttons were leaden bullets.

Second Serv. O wicked cannibal! a fire-lock in 's cod-piece!

First Serv. 'Twas a French plot, upon my life.

Second Serv. To see what the devil can do!

Ant. [Are] all the officers here?

Servants. We are.

Ant. Gentlemen,

We have lost much plate you know; and but this evening
Jewels, to the value of four thousand ducats,
Are missing in the duchess' cabinet.
Are the gates shut?

Serv. Yes.

Ant. 'Tis the duchess' pleasure
Each officer be lock'd into his chamber
Till the sun-rising; and to send the keys
Of all their chests and of their outward doors
Into her bed-chamber. She is very sick.

Rod. At her pleasure.

Ant. She entreats you take't not ill: the innocent
Shall be the more approv'd by it.

Bos. Gentlemen o' the wood-yard, where 's your Switzer now?

First Serv. By this hand, 'twas credibly reported by one o' the black guard.

[*Exeunt all except Antonio and Delio.*

Delio. How fares it with the duchess?

Ant. She 's expos'd
Unto the worst of torture, pain and fear.

Delio. Speak to her all happy comfort.

Ant. How I do play the fool with mine own danger!
You are this night, dear friend, to post to Rome:
My life lies in your service.

Delio. Do not doubt me.

Ant. O, 'tis far from me: and yet fear presents me
Somewhat that looks like danger.
Delio. Believe it,
'Tis but the shadow of your fear, no more:
How superstitiously we mind our evils!
The throwing down salt, or crossing of a hare,
Bleeding at nose, the stumbling of a horse,
Or singing of a cricket, are of power
To daunt whole man in us. Sir, fare you well:
I wish you all the joys of a bless'd father;
And, for my faith, lay this unto your breast,—
Old friends, like old swords, still are trusted best.
[*Exit.*

Enter Cariola.

Cari. Sir, you are the happy father of a son:
Your wife commends him to you.
Ant. Blessèd comfort!—
For heaven' sake, tend her well: I'll presently
Go set a figure for 's nativity. [*Exeunt.*

SCENE III

The court of the same palace.

Enter Bosola, with a dark lantern.

Bos. Sure I did hear a woman shriek: list, ha!
And the sound came, if I receiv'd it right,
From the duchess' lodgings. There's some stratagem

In the confining all our courtiers
To their several wards: I must have part of it;
My intelligence will freeze else. List, again!
It may be 'twas the melancholy bird,
Best friend of silence and of solitariness,
The owl, that screamed so.—Ha! Antonio!

Enter Antonio.

Ant. I heard some noise.—Who's there? what art thou? speak.
Bos. Antonio, put not your face nor body
To such a forc'd expression of fear:
I am Bosola, your friend.
Ant. Bosola!—
[*Aside.*] This mole does undermine me.—Heard you not
A noise even now?
Bos. From whence?
Ant. From the duchess' lodging.
Bos. Not I: did you?
Ant. I did, or else I dream'd.
Bos. Let's walk towards it.
Ant. No: it may be 'twas
But the rising of the wind.
Bos. Very likely.
Methinks 'tis very cold, and yet you sweat:
You look wildly.

Ant. I have been setting a figure
For the duchess' jewels.
Bos. Ah, and how falls your question?
Do you find it radical?
Ant. What 's that to you?
'Tis rather to be question'd what design,
When all men were commanded to their lodgings,
Makes you a night-walker.
Bos. In sooth, I 'll tell you:
Now all the court 's asleep, I thought the devil
Had least to do here; I come to say my prayers;
And if it do offend you I do so,
You are a fine courtier.
Ant. [*aside.*] This fellow will undo me.—
You gave the duchess apricocks to-day:
Pray heaven they were not poison'd!
Bos. Poison'd! a Spanish fig
For the imputation.
Ant. Traitors are ever confident
Till they are discover'd. There were jewels stol'n too:
In my conceit, none are to be suspected
More than yourself.
Bos. You are a false steward.
Ant. Saucy slave, I 'll pull thee up by the roots.
Bos. May be the ruin will crush you to pieces.
Ant. You are an impudent snake indeed, sir:
Are you scarce warm, and do you show your sting?
You libel well, sir.

Bos. No, sir: copy it out,
And I will set my hand to 't.

Ant. [*aside.*] My nose bleeds.
One that were superstitious would count
This ominous, when it merely comes by chance:
Two letters, that are wrote here for my name,
Are drown'd in blood!
Mere accident.—For you, sir, I 'll take order
I' the morn you shall be safe:—[*aside*] 'tis that must colour
Her lying-in:—sir, this door you pass not:
I do not hold it fit that you come near
The duchess' lodgings, till you have quit yourself.—
[*Aside.*] The great are like the base, nay, they are the same,
When they seek shameful ways to avoid shame.
[*Exit.*

Bos. Antonio hereabout did drop a paper:—
Some of your help, false friend:—O, here it is.
What's here? a child's nativity calculated! [*Reads.*
'*The duchess was delivered of a son, 'tween the hours twelve and one in the night, Anno Dom.* 1504,'—that's this year—'*decimo nono Decembris,*'—that's this night—'*taken according to the meridian of Malfi,*'—that's our duchess: happy discovery!—'*The lord of the first house being combust in the ascendant, signifies short life; and Mars being in a human sign, joined to the tail of the*

Dragon, in the eighth house, doth threaten a violent death. Cætera non scrutantur.'
Why, now 'tis most apparent; this precise fellow
Is the duchess' bawd:—I have it to my wish!
This is a parcel of intelligency
Our courtiers were cas'd up for: it needs must follow
That I must be committed on pretence
Of poisoning her; which I'll endure, and laugh at.
If one could find the father now! but that
Time will discover. Old Castruccio
I' the morning posts to Rome: by him I'll send
A letter that shall make her brothers' galls
O'erflow their livers. This was a thrifty way.
Though lust do mask in ne'er so strange disguise,
She's oft found witty, but is never wise. [*Exit.*

SCENE IV

Rome. An apartment in the palace of the Cardinal.

Enter Cardinal and Julia.

Card. Sit: thou art my best of wishes. Prithee, tell me
What trick didst thou invent to come to Rome
Without thy husband?
Julia. Why, my lord, I told him
I came to visit an old anchorite
Here for devotion.
Card. Thou art a witty false one,—
I mean, to him.

Julia. You have prevail'd with me
Beyond my strongest thoughts: I would not now
Find you inconstant.
Card. Do not put thyself
To such a voluntary torture, which proceeds
Out of your own guilt.
Julia. How, my lord!
Card. You fear
My constancy, because you have approv'd
Those giddy and wild turnings in yourself.
Julia. Did you e'er find them?
Card. Sooth, generally for women,
A man might strive to make glass malleable,
Ere he should make them fixèd.
Julia. So, my lord.
Card. We had need go borrow that fantastic glass
Invented by Galileo the Florentine
To view another spacious world i' the moon,
And look to find a constant woman there.
Julia. This is very well, my lord.
Card. Why do you weep?
Are tears your justification? the self-same tears
Will fall into your husband's bosom, lady,
With a loud protestation that you love him
Above the world. Come, I'll love you wisely,
That's jealously; since I am very certain
You cannot make me cuckold.

Julia. I'll go home
To my husband.
Card. You may thank me, lady,
I have taken you off your melancholy perch,
Bore you upon my fist, and show'd you game,
And let you fly at it.—I pray thee, kiss me.—
When thou wast with thy husband, thou wast watched
Like a tame elephant:—still you are to thank me:—
Thou hadst only kisses from him and high feeding;
But what delight was that? 'twas just like one
That hath a little fingering on the lute,
Yet cannot tune it:—still you are to thank me.
Julia. You told me of a piteous wound i' the heart,
And a sick liver, when you woo'd me first,
And spake like one in physic.
Card. Who's that?——

Enter Servant.

Rest firm, for my affection to thee,
Lightning moves slow to 't.
Serv. Madam, a gentleman,
That 's comes post from Malfi, desires to see you.
Card. Let him enter: I'll withdraw. [*Exit.*
Serv. He says
Your husband, old Castruccio, is come to Rome,
Most pitifully tir'd with riding post. [*Exit.*

Enter Delio.

Julia. [*aside.*] Signior Delio! 'tis one of my old suitors.
Delio. I was bold to come and see you.
Julia. Sir, you are welcome.
Delio. Do you lie here?
Julia. Sure, your own experience
Will satisfy you no: our Roman prelates
Do not keep lodging for ladies.
Delio. Very well:
I have brought you no commendations from your husband,
For I know none by him.
Julia. I hear he's come to Rome.
Delio. I never knew man and beast, of a horse and a knight,
So weary of each other: if he had had a good back,
He would have undertook to have borne his horse,
His breech was so pitifully sore.
Julia. Your laughter
Is my pity.
Delio. Lady, I know not whether
You want money, but I have brought you some.
Julia. From my husband?
Delio. No, from mine own allowance.
Julia. I must hear the condition, ere I be bound to take it.
Delio. Look on't, 'tis gold: hath it not a fine colour?

Julia. I have a bird more beautiful.
Delio. Try the sound on 't.
Julia. A lute-string far exceeds it:
It hath no smell, like cassia or civet;
Nor is it physical, though some fond doctors
Persuade us seethe 't in cullises. I 'll tell you,
This is a creature bred by——

Re-enter Servant.

Serv. Your husband 's come,
Hath deliver'd a letter to the Duke of Calabria
That, to my thinking, hath put him out of his wits. [*Exit.*
Julia. Sir, you hear:
Pray, let me know your business and your suit
As briefly as can be.
Delio. With good speed: I would wish you,
At such time as you are non-resident
With your husband, my mistress.
Julia. Sir, I 'll go ask my husband if I shall,
And straight return your answer. [*Exit.*
Delio. Very fine!
Is this her wit, or honesty, that speaks thus?
I heard one say the duke was highly mov'd
With a letter sent from Malfi. I do fear
Antonio is betray'd: how fearfully
Shows his ambition now! unfortunate fortune!

They pass through whirl-pools, and deep woes do shun,
Who the event weigh ere the action's done. [*Exit.*

SCENE V

Another apartment in the same palace.

Enter Cardinal and Ferdinand with a letter.

Ferd. I have this night digg'd up a mandrake.
Card. Say you?
Ferd. And I am grown mad with 't.
Card. What 's the prodigy?
Ferd. Read there,—a sister damn'd: she 's loose i' the hilts;
Grown a notorious strumpet.
Card. Speak lower.
Ferd. Lower!
Rogues do not whisper 't now, but seek to publish 't
(As servants do the bounty of their lords)
Aloud; and with a covetous searching eye,
To mark who note them. O, confusion seize her!
She hath had most cunning bawds to serve her turn,
And more secure conveyances for lust
Than towns of garrison for service.
Card. Is 't possible?
Can this be certain?
Ferd. Rhubarb, O, for rhubarb

To purge this choler! here's the cursèd day
To prompt my memory; and here 't shall stick
Till of her bleeding heart I make a sponge
To wipe it out.

Card. Why do you make yourself
So wild a tempest?

Ferd. Would I could be one,
That I might toss her palace 'bout her ears,
Root up her goodly forests, blast her meads,
And lay her general territory as waste
As she hath done her honours.

Card. Shall our blood,
The royal blood of Arragon and Castile,
Be thus attainted?

Ferd. Apply desperate physic:
We must not now use balsamum, but fire,
The smarting cupping-glass, for that 's the mean
To purge infected blood, such blood as hers.
There is a kind of pity in mine eye,—
I'll give it to my handkercher; and now 'tis here,
I'll bequeath this to her bastard.

Card. What to do?

Ferd. Why, to make soft lint for his mother's wounds,
When I have hew'd her to pieces.

Card. Cursèd creature!
Unequal nature, to place women's hearts
So far upon the left side!

Ferd. Foolish men,

That e'er will trust their honour in a bark
Made of so slight weak bulrush as is woman,
Apt every minute to sink it!

Card. Thus
Ignorance, when it hath purchas'd honour,
It cannot wield it.

Ferd. Methinks I see her laughing,—
Excellent hyena! Talk to me somewhat quickly,
Or my imagination will carry me
To see her in the shameful act of sin.

Card. With whom?

Ferd. Happily with some strong-thigh'd bargeman,
Or one o' the wood-yard that can quoit the sledge
Or toss the bar, or else some lovely squire
That carries coals up to her privy lodgings.

Card. You fly beyond your reason.

Ferd. Go to, mistress!
'Tis not your whore's milk that shall quench my wild-fire,
But your whore's blood.

Card. How idly shows this rage, which carries you,
As men convey'd by witches through the air,
On violent whirlwinds! this intemperate noise
Fitly resembles deaf men's shrill discourse,
Who talk aloud, thinking all other men
To have their imperfection.

Ferd. Have not you
My palsy?

Card. Yes, [but] I can be angry
Without this rupture: there is not in nature
A thing that makes man so deform'd, so beastly,
As doth intemperate anger. Chide yourself.
You have divers men who never yet express'd
Their strong desire of rest but by unrest,
By vexing of themselves. Come, put yourself
In tune.

Ferd. So I will only study to seem
The thing I am not. I could kill her now,
In you, or in myself; for I do think
It is some sin in us heaven doth revenge
By her.

Card. Are you stark mad?

Ferd. I would have their bodies
Burnt in a coal-pit with the ventage stopp'd,
That their curs'd smoke might not ascend to heaven;
Or dip the sheets they lie in in pitch or sulphur,
Wrap them in't, and then light them like a match;
Or else to-boil their bastard to a cullis,
And give't his lecherous father to renew
The sin of his back.

Card. I'll leave you.

Ferd. Nay, I have done.
I am confident, had I been damn'd in hell,

And should have heard of this, it would have put me
Into a cold sweat. In, in ; I 'll go sleep.
Till I know who leaps my sister, I 'll not stir :
That known, I 'll find scorpions to string my whips,
And fix her in a general eclipse. [*Exeunt.*

ACT III

SCENE I

Malfi. An apartment in the palace of the Duchess

Enter Antonio and Delio.

Ant. Our noble friend, my most belovèd Delio !
O, you have been a stranger long at court :
Came you along with the Lord Ferdinand?
Delio. I did, sir : and how fares your noble duchess?
Ant. Right fortunately well : she 's an excellent
Feeder of pedigrees ; since you last saw her,
She hath had two children more, a son and daughter.
Delio. Methinks 'twas yesterday : let me but wink,
And not behold your face, which to mine eye
Is somewhat leaner, verily I should dream
It were within this half hour.
Ant. You have not been in law, friend Delio,
Nor in prison, nor a suitor at the court,
Nor begg'd the reversion of some great man's place,
Nor troubled with an old wife, which doth make
Your time so insensibly hasten.

Delio. Pray, sir, tell me,
Hath not this news arriv'd yet to the ear
Of the lord cardinal?
Ant. I fear it hath:
The Lord Ferdinand, that 's newly come to court,
Doth bear himself right dangerously.
Delio. Pray, why?
Ant. He is so quiet that he seems to sleep
The tempest out, as dormice do in winter:
Those houses that are haunted are most still
Till the devil be up.
Delio. What say the common people?
Ant. The common rabble do directly say
She is a strumpet.
Delio. And your graver heads
Which would be politic, what censure they?
Ant. They do observe I grow to infinite purchase,
The left hand way; and all suppose the duchess
Would amend it, if she could; for, say they,
Great princes, though they grudge their officers
Should have such large and unconfinèd means
To get wealth under them, will not complain,
Lest thereby they should make them odious
Unto the people: for other obligation
Of love or marriage between her and me
They never dream of.
Delio. The Lord Ferdinand
Is going to bed.

Enter Duchess, Ferdinand, and Attendants.

Ferd. I 'll instantly to bed,
For I am weary.—I am to bespeak
A husband for you.
Duch. For me, sir! pray, who is 't?
Ferd. The great Count Malatesti.
Duch. Fie upon him!
A count! he 's a mere stick of sugar-candy;
You may look quite through him. When I choose
A husband, I will marry for your honour.
Ferd. You shall do well in 't.—How is 't, worthy Antonio?
Duch. But, sir, I am to have private conference with you
About a scandalous report is spread
Touching mine honour.
Ferd. Let me be ever deaf to 't:
One of Pasquil's paper-bullets, court-calumny,
A pestilent air, which princes' palaces
Are seldom purg'd of. Yet say that it were true,
I pour it in your bosom, my fix'd love
Would strongly excuse, extenuate, nay, deny
Faults, were they apparent in you. Go, be safe
In your own innocency.
Duch. [*aside*]. O bless'd comfort!
This deadly air is purg'd.
[*Exeunt Duchess, Antonio, Delio, and Attendants.*
Ferd. Her guilt treads on
Hot-burning coulters.

Enter Bosola.

Now, Bosola,
How thrives our intelligence?

Bos. Sir, uncertainly:
'Tis rumour'd she hath had three bastards, but
By whom we may go read i' the stars.

Ferd. Why, some
Hold opinion all things are written there.

Bos. Yes, if we could find spectacles to read them.
I do suspect there hath been some sorcery
Us'd on the duchess.

Ferd. Sorcery! to what purpose?

Bos. To make her dote on some desertless fellow
She shames to acknowledge.

Ferd. Can your faith give way
To think there's power in potions or in charms,
To make us love whether we will or no?

Bos. Most certainly.

Ferd. Away! these are mere gulleries, horrid things,
Invented by some cheating mountebanks
To abuse us. Do you think that herbs or charms
Can force the will? Some trials have been made
In this foolish practice, but the ingredients
Were lenitive poisons, such as are of force
To make the patient mad; and straight the witch
Swears by equivocation they are in love.
The witch-craft lies in her rank blood. This night
I will force confession from her. You told me

You had got, within these two days, a false key
Into her bed-chamber.

Bos. I have.

Ferd. As I would wish.

Bos. What do you intend to do?

Ferd. Can you guess?

Bos. No.

Ferd. Do not ask, then:
He that can compass me, and know my drifts,
May say he hath put a girdle 'bout the world,
And sounded all her quick-sands.

Bos. I do not
Think so.

Ferd. What do you think, then, pray?

Bos. That you are
Your own chronicle too much, and grossly
Flatter yourself.

Ferd. Give me thy hand; I thank thee:
I never gave pension but to flatterers,
Till I entertainèd thee. Farewell.
That friend a great man's ruin strongly checks,
Who rails into his belief all his defects. [*Exeunt.*

SCENE II

The bed-chamber of the Duchess in the same.

Enter Duchess, Antonio, and Cariola.

Duch. Bring me the casket hither, and the glass.—
You get no lodging here to-night, my lord.
Ant. Indeed, I must persuade one.
Duch. Very good :
I hope in time 'twill grow into a custom,
That noblemen shall come with cap and knee
To purchase a night's lodging of their wives.
Ant. I must lie here.
Duch. Must ! you are a lord of mis-rule.
Ant. Indeed, my rule is only in the night.
Duch. To what use will you put me ?
Ant. We'll sleep together.
Duch. Alas,
What pleasure can two lovers find in sleep !
Cari. My lord, I lie with her often ; and I know
She'll much disquiet you.
Ant. See, you are complain'd of.
Cari. For she's the sprawling'st bedfellow.
Ant. I shall like her the better for that.
Cari. Sir, shall I ask you a question ?
Ant. Ay, pray thee, Cariola.

Cari. Wherefore still, when you lie with my lady,
Do you rise so early?
Ant. Labouring men
Count the clock oftenest, Cariola,
Are glad when their task's ended.
Duch. I'll stop your mouth. [*Kisses him.*
Ant. Nay, that's but one; Venus had two soft doves
To draw her chariot; I must have another.—
[*She kisses him again.*
When wilt thou marry, Cariola?
Cari. Never, my lord.
Ant. O, fie upon this single life! forgo it.
We read how Daphne, for her peevish flight,
Became a fruitless bay-tree; Syrinx turn'd
To the pale empty reed; Anaxarete
Was frozen into marble: whereas those
Which married, or prov'd kind unto their friends,
Were by a gracious influence transhap'd
Into the olive, pomegranate, mulberry,
Became flowers, precious stones, or eminent stars.
Cari. This is a vain poetry: but I pray you, tell me,
If there were propos'd me, wisdom, riches, and beauty,
In three several young men, which should I choose?
Ant. 'Tis a hard question: this was Paris' case,
And he was blind in't, and there was a great cause;
For how was't possible he could judge right,
Having three amorous goddesses in view,

And they stark naked? 'twas a motion
Were able to benight the apprehension
Of the severest counsellor of Europe.
Now I look on both your faces so well form'd,
It puts me in mind of a question I would ask.

Cari. What is't?

Ant. I do wonder why hard-favour'd ladies,
For the most part, keep worse-favour'd waiting-women
To attend them, and cannot endure fair ones.

Duch. O, that's soon answer'd.
Did you ever in your life know an ill painter
Desire to have his dwelling next door to the shop
Of an excellent picture-maker? 'twould disgrace
His face-making, and undo him. I prithee,
When were we so merry?—My hair tangles.

Ant. Pray thee, Cariola, let's steal forth the room,
And let her talk to herself: I have divers times
Serv'd her the like, when she hath chaf'd extremely.
I love to see her angry. Softly, Cariola.
[*Exeunt Antonio and Cariola.*

Duch. Doth not the colour of my hair 'gin to change?
When I wax gray, I shall have all the court
Powder their hair with arras, to be like me.
You have cause to love me; I enter'd you into my heart
Before you would vouchsafe to call for the keys.

Enter Ferdinand behind.

We shall one day have my brothers take you napping:
Methinks his presence, being now in court,
Should make you keep your own bed; but you'll say
Love mix'd with fear is sweetest. I 'll assure you,
You shall get no more children till my brothers
Consent to be your gossips. Have you lost your tongue?
'Tis welcome:
For know, whether I am doom'd to live or die,
I can do both like a prince.

Ferd. Die, then, quickly! [*Giving her a poniard.*
Virtue, where art thou hid? what hideous thing
Is it that doth eclipse thee?

Duch. Pray, sir, hear me.

Ferd. Or is it true thou art but a bare name,
And no essential thing?

Duch. Sir——

Ferd. Do not speak.

Duch. No, sir:
I will plant my soul in mine ears, to hear you.

Ferd. O most imperfect light of human reason,
That mak'st us so unhappy to foresee
What we can least prevent! Pursue thy wishes,
And glory in them: there 's in shame no comfort
But to be past all bounds and sense of shame.

Duch. I pray, sir, hear me: I am married.

Ferd. So!

Duch. Happily, not to your liking: but for that,
Alas, your shears do come untimely now
To clip the bird's wings that 's already flown!
Will you see my husband?

Ferd. Yes, if I could change
Eyes with a basilisk.

Duch. Sure, you came hither
By his confederacy.

Ferd. The howling of a wolf
Is music to thee, screech-owl: prithee, peace.—
Whate'er thou art that hast enjoy'd my sister,
For I am sure thou hear'st me, for thine own sake
Let me not know thee. I came hither prepar'd
To work thy discovery; yet am now persuaded
It would beget such violent effects
As would damn us both. I would not for ten millions
I had beheld thee: therefore use all means
I never may have knowledge of thy name;
Enjoy thy lust still, and a wretched life,
On that condition.—And for thee, vile woman,
If thou do wish thy lecher may grow old
In thy embracements, I would have thee build
Such a room for him as our anchorites
To holier use inhabit. Let not the sun
Shine on him till he 's dead; let dogs and monkeys
Only converse with him, and such dumb things
To whom nature denies use to sound his name;
Do not keep a paraquito, lest she learn it;

If thou do love him, cut out thine own tongue,
Lest it bewray him.

Duch. Why might not I marry?
I have not gone about in this to create
Any new world or custom.

Ferd. Thou art undone;
And thou hast ta'en that massy sheet of lead
That hid thy husband's bones, and folded it
About my heart.

Duch. Mine bleeds for 't.

Ferd. Thine! thy heart!
What should I name 't unless a hollow bullet
Fill'd with unquenchable wild-fire?

Duch. You are in this
Too strict; and were you not my princely brother,
I would say, too wilful: my reputation
Is safe.

Ferd. Dost thou know what reputation is?
I 'll tell thee,—to small purpose, since the instruction
Comes now too late.
Upon a time Reputation, Love, and Death,
Would travel o'er the world; and it was concluded
That they should part, and take three several ways.
Death told them, they should find him in great battles,
Or cities plagu'd with plagues: Love gives them counsel
To inquire for him 'mongst unambitious shepherds,
Where dowries were not talk'd of, and sometimes

'Mongst quiet kindred that had nothing left
By their dead parents: 'Stay,' quoth Reputation,
'Do not forsake me; for it is my nature,
If once I part from any man I meet,
I am never found again.' And so for you:
You have shook hands with Reputation,
And made him invisible. So, fare you well:
I will never see you more.

Duch. Why should only I,
Of all the other princes of the world,
Be cas'd up, like a holy relic? I have youth
And a little beauty.

Ferd. So you have some virgins
That are witches. I will never see thee more. [*Exit.*

Re-enter Antonio with a pistol, and Cariola.

Duch. You saw this apparition?

Ant. Yes: we are
Betray'd. How came he hither? I should turn
This to thee, for that.

Cari. Pray, sir, do; and when
That you have cleft my heart, you shall read there
Mine innocence.

Duch. That gallery gave him entrance.

Ant. I would this terrible thing would come again,
That, standing on my guard, I might relate
My warrantable love.— [*She shows the poniard.*
Ha! what means this?

Duch. He left this with me.
Ant. And it seems did wish
You would use it on yourself.
Duch. His action
Seem'd to intend so much.
Ant. This hath a handle to 't,
As well as a point: turn it towards him,
And so fasten the keen edge in his rank gall.
[*Knocking within.*
How now! who knocks? more earthquakes?
Duch. I stand
As if a mine beneath my feet were ready
To be blown up.
Cari. 'Tis Bosola.
Duch. Away!
O misery! methinks unjust actions
Should wear these masks and curtains, and not we.
You must instantly part hence: I have fashion'd it
already. [*Exit Antonio.*

Enter Bosola.

Bos. The duke your brother is ta'en up in a whirlwind;
Hath took horse, and 's rid post to Rome.
Duch. So late?
Bos. He told me, as he mounted into the saddle,
You were undone.
Duch. Indeed, I am very near it.
Bos. What's the matter?

Duch. Antonio, the master of our household,
Hath dealt so falsely with me in 's accounts:
My brother stood engag'd with me for money
Ta'en up of certain Neapolitan Jews,
And Antonio lets the bonds be forfeit.
Bos. Strange!—[*Aside.*] This is cunning.
Duch. And hereupon
My brother's bills at Naples are protested
Against.—Call up our officers.
Bos. I shall. [*Exit.*

Re-enter Antonio.

Duch. The place that you must fly to is Ancona:
Hire a house there; I'll send after you
My treasure and my jewels. Our weak safety
Runs upon enginous wheels: short syllables
Must stand for periods. I must now accuse you
Of such a feignèd crime as Tasso calls
Magnanima menzogna, a noble lie,
'Cause it must shield our honours.—Hark! they are coming.

Re-enter Bosola and Officers.

Ant. Will your grace hear me?
Duch. I have got well by you; you have yielded me
A million of loss: I am like to inherit
The people's curses for your stewardship.
You had the trick in audit-time to be sick,
Till I had signed your quietus; and that cur'd you

Without help of the doctor.—Gentlemen,
I would have this man be an example to you all;
So shall you hold my favour; I pray, let him;
For h'as done that, alas, you would not think of,
And, because I intend to be rid of him,
I mean not to publish.—Use your fortune elsewhere.

Ant. I am strongly arm'd to brook my overthrow,
As commonly men bear with a hard year:
I will not blame the cause on't; but do think
The necessity of my malevolent star
Procures this, not her humour. O, the inconstant
And rotten ground of service! you may see,
'Tis even like him, that in a winter night,
Takes a long slumber o'er a dying fire,
A-loth to part from 't; yet parts thence as cold
As when he first sat down.

Duch. We do confiscate,
Towards the satisfying of your accounts,
All that you have.

Ant. I am all yours; and 'tis very fit
All mine should be so.

Duch. So, sir, you have your pass.

Ant. You may see, gentlemen, what 'tis to serve
A prince with body and soul. [*Exit.*

Bos. Here's an example for extortion: what moisture is drawn out of the sea, when foul weather comes, pours down, and runs into the sea again.

Duch. I would know what are your opinions
Of this Antonio.

Sec. Off. He could not abide to see a pig's head gaping: I thought your grace would find him a Jew.

Third Off. I would you had been his officer, for your own sake.

Fourth Off. You would have had more money.

First Off. He stopped his ears with black wool, and to those came to him for money said he was thick of hearing.

Sec. Off. Some said he was an hermaphrodite, for he could not abide a woman.

Fourth Off. How scurvy proud he would look when the treasury was full! Well, let him go.

First Off. Yes, and the chippings of the buttery fly after him, to scour his gold chain.

Duch. Leave us. [*Exeunt Officers.*
What do you think of these?

Bos. That these are rogues that in 's prosperity,
But to have waited on his fortune, could have wish'd
His dirty stirrup riveted through their noses,
And follow'd after 's mule, like a bear in a ring;
Would have prostituted their daughters to his lust,
Made their first-born intelligencers; thought none happy
But such as were born under his blest planet,
And wore his livery: and do these lice drop off now?

Well, never look to have the like again:
He hath left a sort of flattering rogues behind him;
Their doom must follow. Princes pay flatterers
In their own money: flatterers dissemble their vices,
And they dissemble their lies; that 's justice.
Alas, poor gentleman!

Duch. Poor! he hath amply fill'd his coffers.

Bos. Sure, he was too honest. Pluto, the god of riches,
When he 's sent by Jupiter to any man,
He goes limping, to signify that wealth
That comes on God's name comes slowly; but when he 's sent
On the devil's errand, he rides post and comes in by scuttles.
Let me show you what a most unvalued jewel
You have in a wanton humour thrown away,
To bless the man shall find him. He was an excellent
Courtier and most faithful; a soldier that thought it
As beastly to know his own value too little
As devilish to acknowledge it too much.
Both his virtue and form deserv'd a far better fortune:
His discourse rather delighted to judge itself than show itself:
His breast was filled with all perfection,
And yet it seemed a private whispering-room,
It made so little noise of 't.

Duch. But he was basely descended.

Bos. Will you make yourself a mercenary herald,
Rather to examine men's pedigrees than virtues?
You shall want him:
For know an honest statesman to a prince
Is like a cedar planted by a spring;
The spring bathes the tree's root, the grateful tree
Rewards it with his shadow: you have not done so.
I would sooner swim to the Bermoothes on
Two politicians' rotten bladders, tied
Together with an intelligencer's heart-string,
Than depend on so changeable a prince's favour.
Fare thee well, Antonio! since the malice of the world
Would needs down with thee, it cannot be said yet
That any ill happen'd unto thee, considering thy fall
Was accompanied with virtue.

Duch. O, you render me excellent music!

Bos. Say you?

Duch. This good one that you speak of is my husband.

Bos. Do I not dream? can this ambitious age
Have so much goodness in't as to prefer
A man merely for worth, without these shadows
Of wealth and painted honours? possible?

Duch. I have had three children by him.

Bos. Fortunate lady!
For you have made your private nuptial bed
The humble and fair seminary of peace.

No question but many an unbenefic'd scholar
Shall pray for you for this deed, and rejoice
That some preferment in the world can yet
Arise from merit. The virgins of your land
That have no dowries shall hope your example
Will raise them to rich husbands. Should you want
Soldiers, 'twould make the very Turks and Moors
Turn Christians, and serve you for this act.
Last, the neglected poets of your time,
In honour of this trophy of a man,
Rais'd by that curious engine, your white hand,
Shall thank you, in your grave, for 't; and make that
More reverend than all the cabinets
Of living princes. For Antonio,
His fame shall likewise flow from many a pen,
When heralds shall want coats to sell to men.

Duch. As I taste comfort in this friendly speech,
So would I find concealment.

Bos. O, the secret of my prince,
Which I will wear on the inside of my heart!

Duch. You shall take charge of all my coin and jewels,
And follow him; for he retires himself
To Ancona.

Bos. So.

Duch. Whither, within few days,
I mean to follow thee.

Bos. Let me think:
I would wish your grace to feign a pilgrimage

To our Lady of Loretto, scarce seven leagues
From fair Ancona ; so may you depart
Your country with more honour, and your flight
Will seem a princely progress, retaining
Your usual train about you.

Duch. Sir, your direction
Shall lead me by the hand.

Cari. In my opinion,
She were better progress to the baths at Lucca,
Or go visit the Spa
In Germany ; for, if you will believe me,
I do not like this jesting with religion,
This feigned pilgrimage.

Duch. Thou art a superstitious fool :
Prepare us instantly for our departure.
Past sorrows, let us moderately lament them,
For those to come, seek wisely to prevent them.

[*Exeunt Duchess and Cariola.*

Bos. A politician is the devil's quilted anvil ;
He fashions all sins on him, and the blows
Are never heard : he may work in a lady's chamber,
As here for proof. What rests but I reveal
All to my lord? O, this base quality
Of intelligencer! why, every quality i' the world
Prefers but gain or commendation :
Now, for this act I am certain to be rais'd,
And men that paint weeds to the life are prais'd.

[*Exit.*

SCENE III

An apartment in the Cardinal's palace at Rome.

Enter Cardinal, Ferdinand, Malatesti, Pescara, Delio, and Silvio.

Card. Must we turn soldier, then?
Mal. The emperor,
Hearing your worth that way, ere you attain'd
This reverend garment, joins you in commission
With the right fortunate soldier the Marquis of Pescara,
And the famous Lannoy.
Card. He that had the honour
Of taking the French king prisoner?
Mal. The same.
Here's a plot drawn for a new fortification
At Naples.
Ferd. This great Count Malatesti, I perceive,
Hath got employment?
Delio. No employment, my lord;
A marginal note in the muster-book, that he is
A voluntary lord.
Ferd. He's no soldier.
Delio. He has worn gun-powder in's hollow tooth for the tooth-ache.
Sil. He comes to the leaguer with a full intent
To eat fresh beef and garlic, means to stay
Till the scent be gone, and straight return to court.

Delio. He hath read all the late service
As the City-Chronicle relates it;
And keeps two pewterers going, only to express
Battles in model.
Sil. Then he'll fight by the book.
Delio. By the almanac, I think,
To choose good days and shun the critical;
That's his mistress' scarf.
Sil. Yes, he protests
He would do much for that taffeta.
Delio. I think he would run away from a battle,
To save it from taking prisoner.
Sil. He is horribly afraid
Gun-powder will spoil the perfume on't.
Delio. I saw a Dutchman break his pate once
For calling him pot-gun; he made his head
Have a bore in't like a musket.
Sil. I would he had made a touch-hole to't.
He is indeed a guarded sumpter-cloth,
Only for the remove of the court.

Enter Bosola.

Pes. Bosola arriv'd! what should be the business?
Some falling-out amongst the cardinals.
These factions amongst great men, they are like
Foxes, when their heads are divided,
They carry fire in their tails, and all the country
About them goes to wreck for't.

Sil. What's that Bosola?

Delio. I knew him in Padua,—a fantastical scholar, like such who study to know how many knots was in Hercules' club, of what colour Achilles' beard was, or whether Hector were not troubled with the toothache. He hath studied himself half blear-eyed to know the true symmetry of Cæsar's nose by a shoeing-horn; and this he did to gain the name of a speculative man.

Pes. Mark Prince Ferdinand:
A very salamander lives in 's eye,
To mock the eager violence of fire.

Sil. That cardinal hath made more bad faces with his oppression than ever Michael Angelo made good ones: he lifts up 's nose, like a foul porpoise before a storm.

Pes. The Lord Ferdinand laughs.

Delio. Like a deadly cannon
That lightens ere it smokes.

Pes. These are your true pangs of death,
The pangs of life, that struggle with great statesmen.

Delio. In such a deformed silence witches whisper their charms.

Card. Doth she make religion her riding-hood
To keep her from the sun and tempest?

Ferd. That,
That damns her. Methinks her fault and beauty,
Blended together, show like leprosy,

The whiter, the fouler. I make it a question
Whether her beggarly brats were ever christen'd.
Card. I will instantly solicit the state of Ancona
To have them banish'd.
Ferd. You are for Loretto:
I shall not be at your ceremony; fare you well.—
Write to the Duke of Malfi, my young nephew
She had by her first husband, and acquaint him
With 's mother's honesty. 83
Bos. I will.
Ferd. Antonio!
A slave that only smell'd of ink and counters,
And never in 's life look'd like a gentleman,
But in the audit-time.—Go, go presently,
Draw me out an hundred and fifty of our horse,
And meet me at the foot-bridge. [*Exeunt.*

SCENE IV

Enter Two Pilgrims to the Shrine of our Lady of Loretto.

First Pil. I have not seen a goodlier shrine than this;
Yet I have visited many.
Sec. Pil. The Cardinal of Arragon
Is this day to resign his cardinal's hat:
His sister duchess likewise is arriv'd

To pay her vow of pilgrimage. I expect
A noble ceremony.

First Pil. No question.—They come.

[*Here the ceremony of the Cardinal's instalment, in the habit of a soldier, performed in delivering up his cross, hat, robes, and ring, at the shrine, and investing him with sword, helmet, shield, and spurs; then Antonio, the Duchess, and their children, having presented themselves at the shrine, are, by a form of banishment in dumb-show expressed towards them by the Cardinal and the state of Ancona, banished: during all which ceremony, this ditty is sung, to very solemn music, by divers churchmen: and then exeunt all except the Two Pilgrims.*

Arms and honours deck thy story,
To thy fame's eternal glory!
Adverse fortune ever fly thee;
No disastrous fate come nigh thee!
I alone will sing thy praises,
Whom to honour virtue raises,
And thy study, that divine is,
Bent to martial discipline is,
Lay aside all those robes lie by thee;
Crown thy arts with arms, they'll beautify thee.
O worthy of worthiest name, adorn'd in this manner,
Lead bravely thy forces on under war's warlike banner!

O, mayst thou prove fortunate in all martial courses!
Guide thou still by skill in art and forces!
Victory attend thee nigh, whilst fame sings loud thy powers;
Triumphant conquest crown thy head, and blessings pour down showers!

First Pil. Here's a strange turn of state! who would have thought
So great a lady would have match'd herself
Unto so mean a person? yet the cardinal
Bears himself much too cruel.

Sec. Pil. They are banish'd.

First Pil. But I would ask what power hath this state
Of Ancona to determine of a free prince?

Sec. Pil. They are a free state, sir, and her brother show'd
How that the Pope, fore-hearing of her looseness,
Hath seiz'd into the protection of the church
The dukedom which she held as dowager.

First Pil. But by what justice?

Sec. Pil. Sure, I think by none,
Only her brother's instigation.

First Pil. What was it with such violence he took
Off from her finger?

Sec. Pil. 'Twas her wedding-ring;
Which he vow'd shortly he would sacrifice
To his revenge.

First Pil. Alas, Antonio!
If that a man be thrust into a well,
No matter who sets hand to't, his own weight

Will bring him sooner to the bottom. Come, let 's
hence.
Fortune makes this conclusion general,
All things do help the unhappy man to fall.
[*Exeunt.*

SCENE V

Near Loretto.

Enter Duchess, Antonio, Children, Cariola, and Servants.

Duch. Banish'd Ancona!
Ant. Yes, you see what power
Lightens in great men's breath.
Duch. Is all our train
Shrunk to this poor remainder?
Ant. These poor men,
Which have got little in your service, vow
To take your fortune: but your wiser buntings,
Now they are fledg'd, are gone.
Duch. They have done wisely.
This puts me in mind of death: physicians thus,
With their hands full of money, use to give o'er
Their patients.
Ant. Right the fashion of the world:
From decay'd fortunes every flatterer shrinks;
Men cease to build where the foundation sinks.
Duch. I had a very strange dream to-night.

Ant. What was't?
Duch. Methought I wore my coronet of state,
And on a sudden all the diamonds
Were chang'd to pearls.
Ant. My interpretation
Is, you'll weep shortly; for to me the pearls
Do signify your tears.
Duch. The birds that live i' the field
On the wild benefit of nature live
Happier than we; for they may choose their mates,
And carol their sweet pleasures to the spring.

Enter Bosola with a letter.

Bos. You are happily o'erta'en.
Duch. From my brother?
Bos. Yes, from the Lord Ferdinand your brother
All love and safety.
Duch. Thou dost blanch mischief,
Would'st make it white. See, see, like to calm weather
At sea before a tempest, false hearts speak fair
To those they intend most mischief. [*Reads.*
'*Send Antonio to me; I want his head in a business.*'
A politic equivocation!
He doth not want your counsel, but your head;
That is, he cannot sleep till you be dead.
And here's another pitfall that's strew'd o'er
With roses; mark it, 'tis a cunning one: [*Reads.*

'I stand engaged for your husband for several debts at Naples: let not that trouble him; I had rather have his heart than his money' :—
And I believe so too.

Bos. What do you believe?

Duch. That he so much distrusts my husband's love,
He will by no means believe his heart is with him
Until he see it: the devil is not cunning enough
To circumvent us in riddles.

Bos. Will you reject that noble and free league
Of amity and love which I present you?

Duch. Their league is like that of some politic kings,
Only to make themselves of strength and power
To be our after-ruin; tell them so.

Bos. And what from you?

Ant. Thus tell him; I will not come.

Bos. And what of this?

Ant. My brothers have dispers'd
Bloodhounds abroad; which till I hear are muzzled,
No truce, though hatch'd with ne'er such politic skill,
Is safe, that hangs upon our enemies' will.
I'll not come at them.

Bos. This proclaims your breeding:
Every small thing draws a base mind to fear,
As the adamant draws iron. Fare you well, sir:
You shall shortly hear from 's. [*Exit.*

Duch. I suspect some ambush:

Therefore by all my love I do conjure you
To take your eldest son, and fly towards Milan.
Let us not venture all this poor remainder
In one unlucky bottom.

Ant. You counsel safely.
Best of my life, farewell, since we must part:
Heaven hath a hand in 't; but no otherwise
Than as some curious artist takes in sunder
A clock or watch, when it is out of frame,
To bring 't in better order.

Duch. I know not which is best,
To see you dead, or part with you.—Farewell, boy:
Thou art happy that thou hast not understanding
To know thy misery; for all our wit
And reading brings us to a truer sense
Of sorrow.—In the eternal church, sir,
I do hope we shall not part thus.

Ant. O, be of comfort!
Make patience a noble fortitude,
And think not how unkindly we are us'd:
Man, like to cassia, is prov'd best, being bruis'd.

Duch. Must I, like to a slave-born Russian,
Account it praise to suffer tyranny?
And yet, O heaven, thy heavy hand is in 't!
I have seen my little boy oft scourge his top,
And compared myself to 't: naught made me e'er
Go right but heaven's scourge-stick.

Ant. Do not weep:
Heaven fashion'd us of nothing; and we strive
To bring ourselves to nothing.—Farewell, Cariola,
And thy sweet armful.—If I do never see thee more,
Be a good mother to your little ones,
And save them from the tiger: fare you well.
Duch. Let me look upon you once more, for that speech
Came from a dying father: your kiss is colder
Than that I have seen an holy anchorite
Give to a dead man's skull.
Ant. My heart is turn'd to a heavy lump of lead,
With which I sound my danger: fare you well.
[*Exeunt Antonio and his son.*
Duch. My laurel is all wither'd.
Cari. Look, madam, what a troop of armèd men
Make toward us!
Duch. O, they are very welcome:
When Fortune's wheel is over-charg'd with princes,
The weight makes it move swift: I would have my ruin
Be sudden.

Re-enter Bosola visarded, with a Guard.

I am your adventure, am I not?
Bos. You are: you must see your husband no more.
Duch. What devil art thou that counterfeit'st heaven's thunder?
Bos. Is that terrible? I would have you tell me whether

Is that note worse that frights the silly birds
Out of the corn, or that which doth allure them
To the nets? you have hearken'd to the last too much.

Duch. O misery! like to a rusty o'ercharg'd cannon,
Shall I never fly in pieces?—Come, to what prison?

Bos. To none.

Duch. Whither, then?

Bos. To your palace.

Duch. I have heard
That Charon's boat serves to convey all o'er
The dismal lake, but brings none back again.

Bos. Your brothers mean you safety and pity.

Duch. Pity!
With such a pity men preserve alive
Pheasants and quails, when they are not fat enough
To be eaten.

Bos. These are your children?

Duch. Yes.

Bos. Can they prattle?

Duch. No:
But I intend, since they were born accurs'd,
Curses shall be their first language.

Bos. Fie, madam!
Forget this base, low fellow——

Duch. Were I a man,
I 'd beat that counterfeit face into thy other.

Bos. One of no birth.

Duch. Say that he was born mean,
Man is most happy when 's own actions
Be arguments and examples of his virtue.
Bos. A barren, beggarly virtue.
Duch. I prithee, who is greatest? can you tell?
Sad tales befit my woe: I 'll tell you one.
A salmon, as she swam unto the sea,
Met with a dog-fish, who encounters her
With this rough language; 'Why art thou so bold
To mix thyself with our high state of floods,
Being no eminent courtier, but one
That for the calmest and fresh time o' the year
Dost live in shallow rivers, rank'st thyself
With silly smelts and shrimps? and darest thou
Pass by our dog-ship without reverence?'
'O,' quoth the salmon, 'sister, be at peace:
Thank Jupiter we both have pass'd the net!
Our value never can be truly known,
Till in the fisher's basket we be shown:
I' the market then my price may be the higher,
Even when I am nearest to the cook and fire.'
So to great men the moral may be stretch'd;
Men oft are valu'd high, when they're most wretch'd.—
But come, whither you please. I am arm'd 'gainst misery;
Bent to all sways of the oppressor's will:
There 's no deep valley but near some great hill.
[*Exeunt.*

ACT IV

SCENE I

Malfi. An apartment in the palace of the Duchess.

Enter Ferdinand and Bosola.

Ferd. How doth our sister duchess bear herself
In her imprisonment?
Bos. Nobly: I'll describe her.
She's sad as one long us'd to't, and she seems
Rather to welcome the end of misery
Than shun it; a behaviour so noble
As gives a majesty to adversity:
You may discern the shape of loveliness
More perfect in her tears than in her smiles:
She will muse for hours together; and her silence,
Methinks, expresseth more than if she spake.
Ferd. Her melancholy seems to be fortified
With a strange disdain.
Bos. 'Tis so; and this restraint,
Like English mastives that grow fierce with tying,
Makes her too passionately apprehend
Those pleasures she's kept from.

Ferd. Curse upon her!
I will no longer study in the book
Of another's heart. Inform her what I told you.
[*Exit.*

Enter Duchess.

Bos. All comfort to your grace!
Duch. I will have none.
Pray thee, why dost thou wrap thy poison'd pills
In gold and sugar?
Bos. Your elder brother, the Lord Ferdinand,
Is come to visit you, and sends you word,
'Cause once he rashly made a solemn vow
Never to see you more, he comes i' the night;
And prays you gently neither torch nor taper
Shine in your chamber: he will kiss your hand,
And reconcile himself; but for his vow
He dares not see you.
Duch. At his pleasure.—
Take hence the lights.—He 's come.

Enter Ferdinand.

Ferd. Where are you?
Duch. Here, sir.
Ferd. This darkness suits you well.
Duch. I would ask you pardon.
Ferd. You have it;
For I account it the honorabl'st revenge,

Where I may kill, to pardon.—Where are your cubs?

Duch. Whom?

Ferd. Call them your children;
For though our national law distinguish bastards
From true legitimate issue, compassionate nature
Makes them all equal.

Duch. Do you visit me for this?
You violate a sacrament o' the church
Shall make you howl in hell for 't.

Ferd. It had been well,
Could you have liv'd thus always; for, indeed,
You were too much i' the light:—but no more;
I come to seal my peace with you. Here 's a hand
[*Gives her a dead man's hand.*
To which you have vow'd much love; the ring upon 't
You gave.

Duch. I affectionately kiss it.

Ferd. Pray, do, and bury the print of it in your heart.
I will leave this ring with you for a love-token;
And the hand as sure as the ring; and do not doubt
But you shall have the heart too: when you need a friend,
Send it to him that ow'd it; you shall see
Whether he can aid you.

Duch. You are very cold:

I fear you are not well after your travel.—
Ha! lights!——O, horrible!

Ferd. Let her have lights enough. [*Exit.*

Duch. What witchcraft doth he practise, that he hath left
A dead man's hand here.

[*Here is discovered, behind a traverse, the artificial figures of Antonio and his children, appearing as if they were dead.*

Bos. Look you, here's the piece from which 'twas ta'en.
He doth present you this sad spectacle,
That, now you know directly they are dead,
Hereafter you may wisely cease to grieve
For that which cannot be recoverèd.

Duch. There is not between heaven and earth one wish
I stay for after this: it wastes me more
Than were't my picture, fashion'd out of wax,
Stuck with a magical needle, and then buried
In some foul dunghill; and yond's an excellent property
For a tyrant, which I would account mercy.

Bos. What's that?

Duch. If they would bind me to that lifeless trunk,
And let me freeze to death.

Bos. Come, you must live.

Duch. That's the greatest torture souls feel in hell,
In hell, that they must live, and cannot die.
Portia, I'll new kindle thy coals again,

And revive the rare and almost dead example
Of a loving wife.

Bos. O, fie! despair? remember
You are a Christian.

Duch. The church enjoins fasting:
I'll starve myself to death.

Bos. Leave this vain sorrow.
Things being at the worst begin to mend: the bee
When he hath shot his sting into your hand,
May then play with your eye-lid.

Duch. Good comfortable fellow,
Persuade a wretch that's broke upon the wheel
To have all his bones new set; entreat him live
To be executed again. Who must despatch me?
I account this world a tedious theatre,
For I do play a part in 't 'gainst my will.

Bos. Come, be of comfort; I will save your life.

Duch. Indeed, I have not leisure to tend
So small a business.

Bos. Now, by my life, I pity you.

Duch. Thou art a fool, then,
To waste thy pity on a thing so wretched
As cannot pity itself. I am full of daggers.
Puff, let me blow these vipers from me.

Enter Servant.

What are you?

Serv. One that wishes you long life.

Duch. I would thou wert hang'd for the horrible curse
Thou hast given me: I shall shortly grow one
Of the miracles of pity. I 'll go pray;—
No, I 'll go curse.

Bos. O, fie!

Duch. I could curse the stars.

Bos. O, fearful!

Duch. And those three smiling seasons of the year
Into a Russian winter: nay, the world
To its first chaos.

Bos. Look you, the stars shine still.

Duch. O, but you must
Remember, my curse hath a great way to go.—
Plagues, that make lanes through largest families,
Consume them!—

Bos. Fie, lady!

Duch. Let them, like tyrants,
Never be remember'd but for the ill they have done;
Let all the zealous prayers of mortified
Churchmen forget them!—

Bos. O, uncharitable!

Duch. Let heaven a little while cease crowning martyrs,
To punish them!—
Go, howl them this, and say, I long to bleed:
It is some mercy when men kill with speed.

[*Exit.*

Re-enter Ferdinand.

Ferd. Excellent, as I would wish; she's plagu'd in art:
These presentations are but fram'd in wax
By the curious master in that quality,
Vincentio Lauriola, and she takes them
For true substantial bodies.
Bos. Why do you do this?
Ferd. To bring her to despair.
Bos. Faith, end here,
And go no farther in your cruelty:
Send her a penitential garment to put on
Next to her delicate skin, and furnish her
With beads and prayer-books.
Ferd. Damn her! that body of hers,
While that my blood ran pure in 't, was more worth
Than that which thou wouldst comfort, call'd a soul.
I will send her masks of common courtezans,
Have her meat serv'd up by bawds and ruffians,
And, 'cause she 'll needs be mad, I am resolv'd
To move forth the common hospital
All the mad-folk, and place them near her lodging;
There let them practise together, sing and dance,
And act their gambols to the full o' the moon:
If she can sleep the better for it, let her.
Your work is almost ended.
Bos. Must I see her again?
Ferd. Yes.

Bos. Never.
Ferd. You must.
Bos. Never in mine own shape;
That 's forfeited by my intelligence
And this last cruel lie: when you send me next,
The business shall be comfort.
Ferd. Very likely;
Thy pity is nothing of kin to thee. Antonio
Lurks about Milan: thou shalt shortly thither,
To feed a fire as great as my revenge,
Which never will slack till it hath spent his fuel:
Intemperate agues make physicians cruel. [*Exeunt.*

SCENE II

Another room in the lodging of the Duchess.

Enter Duchess and Cariola.

Duch. What hideous noise was that?
Cari. 'Tis the wild consort
Of madmen, lady, which your tyrant brother
Hath plac'd about your lodging: this tyranny,
I think, was never practis'd till this hour.
Duch. Indeed, I thank him: nothing but noise and folly
Can keep me in my right wits; whereas reason
And silence make me stark mad. Sit down;
Discourse to me some dismal tragedy.
Cari. O, 'twill increase your melancholy!

Duch. Thou art deceiv'd:
To hear of greater grief would lessen mine.
This is a prison?
Cari. Yes, but you shall live
To shake this durance off.
Duch. Thou art a fool:
The robin-red-breast and the nightingale
Never live long in cages.
Cari. Pray, dry your eyes.
What think you of, madam?
Duch. Of nothing;
When I muse thus, I sleep.
Cari. Like a madman, with your eyes open?
Duch. Dost thou think we shall know one another
In the other world?
Cari. Yes, out of question.
Duch. O, that it were possible we might
But hold some two days' conference with the dead!
From them I should learn somewhat, I am sure,
I never shall know here. I 'll tell thee a miracle;
I am not mad yet, to my cause of sorrow:
The heaven o'er my head seems made of molten brass,
The earth of flaming sulphur, yet I am not mad.
I am acquainted with sad misery
As the tann'd galley-slave is with his oar;
Necessity makes me suffer constantly,
And custom makes it easy. Who do I look like now?

Cari. Like to your picture in the gallery,
A deal of life in show, but none in practice;
Or rather like some reverend monument
Whose ruins are even pitied.
Duch. Very proper;
And Fortune seems only to have her eye-sight
To behold my tragedy.—How now!
What noise is that?

Enter Servant.

Serv. I am come to tell you
Your brother hath intended you some sport.
A great physician, when the Pope was sick
Of a deep melancholy, presented him
With several sorts of madmen, which wild object
Being full of change and sport, forc'd him to laugh,
And so the imposthume broke: the self-same cure
The duke intends on you.
Duch. Let them come in.
Serv. There's a mad lawyer; and a secular priest;
A doctor that hath forfeited his wits
By jealousy; an astrologian
That in his works said such a day o' the month
Should be the day of doom, and, failing of't,
Ran mad; an English tailor craz'd i' the brain
With the study of new fashions; a gentleman-usher
Quite beside himself with care to keep in mind
The number of his lady's salutations

Or 'How do you' she employ'd him in each morning;
A farmer, too, an excellent knave in grain,
Mad 'cause he was hinder'd transportation:
And let one broker that's mad loose to these,
You'd think the devil were among them.
Duch. Sit, Cariola.—Let them loose when you please,
For I am chain'd to endure all your tyranny.

Enter Madmen.

Here by a Madman this song is sung to a dismal kind of music.

O, let us howl some heavy note,
Some deadly doggèd howl,
Sounding as from the threatening throat
Of beasts and fatal fowl!
As ravens, screech-owls, bulls, and bears,
We'll bell, and bawl our parts,
Till irksome noise have cloy'd your ears
And córrosiv'd your hearts.
At last, whenas our quire wants breath,
Our bodies being blest,
We'll sing, like swans, to welcome death,
And die in love and rest.

First Maaman. Doom's-day not come yet! I'll draw it nearer by a perspective, or make a glass that shall set all the world on fire upon an instant. I cannot sleep; my pillow is stuffed with a litter of porcupines.

Second Madman. Hell is a mere glass-house, where the devils are continually blowing up women's souls on hollow irons, and the fire never goes out.

Third Madman. I will lie with every woman in my parish the tenth night; I will tythe them over like hay-cocks.

Fourth Madman. Shall my pothecary out-go me because I am a cuckold? I have found out his roguery; he makes allum out of his wife's urine, and sells it to Puritans that have sore throats with over-straining.

First Madman. I have skill in heraldry.

Second Madman. Hast?

First Madman. You do give for your crest a woodcock's head with the brains picked out on't; you are a very ancient gentleman.

Third Madman. Greek is turned Turk: we are only to be saved by the Helvetian translation.

First Madman. Come on, sir, I will lay the law to you.

Second Madman. O, rather lay a corrosive: the law will eat to the bone.

Third Madman. He that drinks but to satisfy nature is damned.

Fourth Madman. If I had my glass here, I would show a sight should make all the women here call me mad doctor.

First Madman. What's he? a rope-maker?

Second Madman. No, no, no, a snuffling knave that, while he shows the tombs, will have his hand in a wench's placket.

Third Madman. Woe to the caroche that brought home my wife from the mask at three o'clock in the morning! it had a large featherbed in it.

Fourth Madman. I have pared the devil's nails forty times, roasted them in raven's eggs, and cured agues with them.

Third Madman. Get me three hundred milch-bats, to make possets to procure sleep.

Fourth Madman. All the college may throw their caps at me: I have made a soap-boiler costive; it was my masterpiece.

[*Here the dance, consisting of Eight Madmen, with music answerable thereunto; after which, Bosola, like an old man, enters.*

Duch. Is he mad too?

Serv. Pray, question him. I'll leave you.

[*Exeunt Servant and Madmen.*

Bos. I am come to make thy tomb.

Duch. Ha! my tomb!
Thou speak'st as if I lay upon my death-bed,
Gasping for breath: dost thou perceive me sick?

Bos. Yes, and the more dangerously, since thy sickness is insensible.

Duch. Thou art not mad, sure: dost know me?

Bos. Yes.

Duch. Who am I?

Bos. Thou art a box of worm-seed, at best but a salvatory of green mummy. What's this flesh? a little crudded milk, fantastical puff-paste. Our bodies are weaker than those paper-prisons boys use to keep flies in; more contemptible, since ours is to preserve earth-worms. Didst thou ever see a lark in a cage? Such is the soul in the body: this world is like her little turf of grass, and the heaven o'er our heads like her looking-glass, only gives us a miserable knowledge of the small compass of our prison.

Duch. Am not I thy duchess?

Bos. Thou art some great woman, sure, for riot begins to sit on thy forehead (clad in gray hairs) twenty years sooner than on a merry milk-maid's. Thou sleepest worse than if a mouse should be forced to take up her lodging in a cat's ear: a little infant that breeds its teeth, should it lie with thee, would cry out, as if thou wert the more unquiet bedfellow.

Duch. I am Duchess of Malfi still.

Bos. That makes thy sleep so broken:
Glories, like glow-worms, afar off shine bright,
But, look'd to near, have neither heat nor light.

Duch. Thou art very plain.

Bos. My trade is to flatter the dead, not the living; I am a tomb-maker.

Duch. And thou comest to make my tomb?

Bos. Yes.

Duch. Let me be a little merry:—of what stuff wilt thou make it?

Bos. Nay, resolve me first, of what fashion?

Duch. Why, do we grow fantastical on our deathbed? do we affect fashion in the grave?

Bos. Most ambitiously. Princes' images on their tombs do not lie, as they were wont, seeming to pray up to heaven; but with their hands under their cheeks, as if they died of the tooth-ache: they are not carved with their eyes fixed upon the stars; but as their minds were wholly bent upon the world, the self-same way they seem to turn their faces.

Duch. Let me know fully therefore the effect
Of this thy dismal preparation,
This talk fit for a charnel.

Bos. Now I shall:—

Enter Executioners, with a coffin, cords, and a bell.

Here is a present from your princely brothers;
And may it arrive welcome, for it brings
Last benefit, last sorrow.

Duch. Let me see it:
I have so much obedience in my blood,
I wish it in their veins to do them good.

Bos. This is your last presence-chamber.

Cari. O my sweet lady!

Duch. Peace; it affrights not me.

Bos. I am the common bellman

That usually is sent to condemn'd persons
The night before they suffer.

Duch. Even now thou said'st
Thou wast a tomb-maker.

Bos. 'Twas to bring you
By degrees to mortification. Listen.

Hark, now everything is still,
The screech-owl and the whistler shrill
Call upon our dame aloud,
And bid her quickly don her shroud!
Much you had of land and rent;
Your length in clay's now competent:
A long war disturb'd your mind;
Here your perfect peace is sign'd.
Of what is't fools make such vain keeping?
Sin their conception, their birth weeping,
Their life a general mist of error,
Their death a hideous storm of terror.
Strew your hair with powders sweet,
Don clean linen, bathe your feet,
And (the foul fiend more to check)
A crucifix let bless your neck:
'Tis now full tide 'tween night and day;
End your groan, and come away.

Cari. Hence, villains, tyrants, murderers! alas!
What will you do with my lady?—Call for help.

Duch. To whom? to our next neighbours? they are mad-folks.

Bos. Remove that noise.
Duch. Farewell, Cariola.
In my last will I have not much to give:
A many hungry guests have fed upon me;
Thine will be a poor reversion.
Cari. I will die with her.
Duch. I pray thee, look thou giv'st my little boy
Some syrup for his cold, and let the girl
Say her prayers ere she sleep.
[*Cariola is forced out by the Executioners.*
Now what you please:
What death?
Bos. Strangling; here are your executioners.
Duch. I forgive them:
The apoplexy, catarrh, or cough o' the lungs,
Would do as much as they do.
Bos. Doth not death fright you?
Duch. Who would be afraid on't,
Knowing to meet such excellent company
In the other world?
Bos. Yet, methinks,
The manner of your death should much afflict you:
This cord should terrify you.
Duch. Not a whit:
What would it pleasure me to have my throat cut
With diamonds? or to be smothered
With cassia? or to be shot to death with pearls?
I know death hath ten thousand several doors

For men to take their exits; and 'tis found
They go on such strange geometrical hinges,
You may open them both ways: any way, for heaven-sake,
So I were out of your whispering. Tell my brothers
That I perceive death, now I am well awake,
Best gift is they can give or I can take.
I would fain put off my last woman's fault,
I'd not be tedious to you.

First Execut. We are ready.

Duch. Dispose my breath how please you; but my body
Bestow upon my women, will you?

First Execut. Yes.

Duch. Pull, and pull strongly, for your able strength
Must pull down heaven upon me:—
Yet stay; heaven-gates are not so highly arch'd
As princes' palaces; they that enter there
Must go upon their knees [*Kneels*].—Come, violent death,
Serve for mandragora to make me sleep!—
Go tell my brothers, when I am laid out,
They then may feed in quiet.

[*The Executioners strangle the Duchess.*

Bos. Where's the waiting-woman?
Fetch her: some other strangle the children.

[*Cariola and Children are brought in by the Executioners; who presently strangle the Children.*

Look you, there sleeps your mistress.

Cari. O, you are damn'd
Perpetually for this! My turn is next;
Is 't not so order'd?
Bos. Yes, and I am glad
You are so well prepar'd for 't.
Cari. You are deceiv'd, sir,
I am not prepar'd for 't, I will not die;
I will first come to my answer, and know
How I have offended.
Bos. Come, despatch her.—
You kept her counsel; now you shall keep ours.
Cari. I will not die, I must not; I am contracted
To a young gentleman.
First Execut. Here 's your wedding-ring.
Cari. Let me but speak with the duke. I 'll discover
Treason to his person.
Bos. Delays:—throttle her.
First Execut. She bites and scratches.
Cari. If you kill me now,
I am damn'd; I have not been at confession
This two years.
Bos. [*to Executioners.*] When?
Cari. I am quick with child.
Bos. Why, then,
Your credit 's saved. [*Executioners strangle Cariola.*
Bear her into the next room;
Let these lie still.
[*Exeunt the Executioners with the body of Cariola.*

Enter Ferdinand.

Ferd. Is she dead?

Bos. She is what
You'd have her. But here begin your pity:
[*Shows the Children strangled.*
Alas, how have these offended?

Ferd. The death
Of young wolves is never to be pitied.

Bos. Fix your eye here.

Ferd. Constantly.

Bos. Do you not weep?
Other sins only speak; murder shrieks out:
The element of water moistens the earth,
But blood flies upwards and bedews the heavens.

Ferd. Cover her face; mine eyes dazzle: she died young.

Bos. I think not so; her infelicity
Seem'd to have years too many.

Ferd. She and I were twins;
And should I die this instant, I had liv'd
Her time to a minute.

Bos. It seems she was born first:
You have bloodily approv'd the ancient truth,
That kindred commonly do worse agree
Than remote strangers.

Ferd. Let me see her face
Again. Why didst thou not pity her? what
An excellent honest man mightst thou have been,
If thou hadst borne her to some sanctuary!

Or, bold in a good cause, oppos'd thyself,
With thy advancèd sword above thy head,
Between her innocence and my revenge!
I bade thee, when I was distracted of my wits,
Go kill my dearest friend, and thou hast done't.
For let me but examine well the cause:
What was the meanness of her match to me?
Only I must confess I had a hope,
Had she continu'd widow, to have gain'd
An infinite mass of treasure by her death:
And what was the main cause? her marriage,
That drew a stream of gall quite through my heart.
For thee, as we observe in tragedies
That a good actor many times is curs'd
For playing a villain's part, I hate thee for't,
And, for my sake, say, thou hast done much ill well.

Bos. Let me quicken your memory, for I perceive
You are falling into ingratitude: I challenge
The reward due to my service.

Ferd. I'll tell thee
What I'll give thee.

Bos. Do.

Ferd. I'll give thee a pardon
For this murder.

Bos. Ha!

Ferd. Yes, and 'tis

The largest bounty I can study to do thee.
By what authority didst thou execute
This bloody sentence?

Bos. By yours.

Ferd. Mine! was I her judge?
Did any ceremonial form of law
Doom her to not-being? did a cómplete jury
Deliver her conviction up i' the court?
Where shalt thou find this judgment register'd,
Unless in hell? See, like a bloody fool,
Thou 'st forfeited thy life, and thou shalt die for 't.

Bos. The office of justice is perverted quite
When one thief hangs another. Who shall dare
To reveal this?

Ferd. O, I 'll tell thee;
The wolf shall find her grave, and scrape it up,
Not to devour the corpse, but to discover
The horrid murder.

Bos. You, not I, shall quake for 't.

Ferd. Leave me.

Bos. I will first receive my pension.

Ferd. You are a villain.

Bos. When your ingratitude
Is judge, I am so.

Ferd. O horror,
That not the fear of him which binds the devils
Can prescribe man obedience!—
Never look upon me more.

Bos. Why, fare thee well.
Your brother and yourself are worthy men:
You have a pair of hearts are hollow graves,
Rotten, and rotting others; and your vengeance,
Like two chain'd bullets, still goes arm in arm:
You may be brothers; for treason, like the plague,
Doth take much in a blood. I stand like one
That long hath ta'en a sweet and golden dream:
I am angry with myself, now that I wake.
Ferd. Get thee into some unknown part o' the world,
That I may never see thee.
Bos. Let me know
Wherefore I should be thus neglected. Sir,
I serv'd your tyranny, and rather strove
To satisfy yourself than all the world:
And though I loath'd the evil, yet I lov'd
You that did counsel it; and rather sought
To appear a true servant than an honest man.
Ferd. I 'll go hunt the badger by owl-light:
'Tis a deed of darkness. [*Exit.*
Bos. He 's much distracted. Off, my painted honour!
While with vain hopes our faculties we tire,
We seem to sweat in ice and freeze in fire.
What would I do, were this to do again?
I would not change my peace of conscience
For all the wealth of Europe.—She stirs; here's life:—
Return, fair soul, from darkness, and lead mine

Out of this sensible hell:—she's warm, she breathes:—
Upon thy pale lips I will melt my heart,
To store them with fresh colour.—Who's there!
Some cordial drink!—Alas! I dare not call:
So pity would destroy pity.—Her eye opes,
And heaven in it seems to ope, that late was shut,
To take me up to mercy.

Duch. Antonio!

Bos. Yes, madam, he is living;
The dead bodies you saw were but feign'd statues:
He's reconcil'd to your brothers; the Pope hath wrought
The atonement.

Duch. Mercy! [*Dies.*

Bos. O, she's gone again! there the cords of life broke.
O sacred innocence, that sweetly sleeps
On turtles' feathers, whilst a guilty conscience
Is a black register wherein is writ
All our good deeds and bad, a perspective
That shows us hell! That we cannot be suffer'd
To do good when we have a mind to it!
This is manly sorrow;
These tears, I am very certain, never grew
In my mother's milk: my estate is sunk
Below the degree of fear: where were
These penitent fountains while she was living?
O, they were frozen up! Here is a sight

As direful to my soul as is the sword
Unto a wretch hath slain his father. Come,
I 'll bear thee hence,
And execute thy last will; that 's deliver
Thy body to the reverend dispose
Of some good women: that the cruel tyrant
Shall not deny me. Then I 'll post to Milan,
Where somewhat I will speedily enact
Worth my dejection. [*Exit.*

ACT V

SCENE I

Milan. A public place.

Enter Antonio and Delio.

Ant. What think you of my hope of reconcilement
To the Arragonian brethren?
Delio. I misdoubt it;
For though they have sent their letters of safe-conduct
For your repair to Milan, they appear
But nets to entrap you. The Marquis of Pescara,
Under whom you hold certain land in cheat,
Much 'gainst his noble nature hath been mov'd
To seize those lands; and some of his dependants
Are at this instant making it their suit
To be invested in your revenues.
I cannot think they mean well to your life
That do deprive you of your means of life,
Your living.
Ant. You are still an heretic
To any safety I can shape myself.

Delio. Here comes the marquis: I will make myself
Petitioner for some part of your land,
To know whither it is flying.
Ant. I pray, do.

Enter Pescara.

Delio. Sir, I have a suit to you.
Pes. To me?
Delio. An easy one:
There is the Citadel of Saint Bennet,
With some demesnes, of late in the possession
Of Antonio Bologna,—please you bestow them on me.
Pes. You are my friend; but this is such a suit,
Nor fit for me to give, nor you to take.
Delio. No, sir?
Pes. I will give you ample reason for't
Soon in private:—here's the cardinal's mistress.

Enter Julia.

Julia. My lord, I am grown your poor petitioner,
And should be an ill beggar, had I not
A great man's letter here, the cardinal's,
To court you in my favour. [*Gives a letter.*
Pes. He entreats for you
The Citadel of Saint Bennet, that belong'd
To the banish'd Bologna.
Julia. Yes.

Pes. I could not have thought of a friend I could rather
Pleasure with it: 'tis yours.
Julia. Sir, I thank you;
And he shall know how doubly I am engag'd
Both in your gift, and speediness of giving
Which makes your grant the greater. [*Exit.*
Ant. How they fortify
Themselves with my ruin!
Delio. Sir, I am
Little bound to you.
Pes. Why?
Delio. Because you denied this suit to me, and gave 't
To such a creature.
Pes. Do you know what it was?
It was Antonio's land; not forfeited
By course of law, but ravish'd from his throat
By the cardinal's entreaty: it were not fit
I should bestow so main a piece of wrong
Upon my friend; 'tis a gratification
Only due to a strumpet, for it is injustice.
Shall I sprinkle the pure blood of innocents
To make those followers I call my friends
Look ruddier upon me? I am glad
This land, ta'en from the owner by such wrong,
Returns again unto so foul an use
As salary for his lust. Learn, good Delio,
To ask noble things of me, and you shall find
I 'll be a noble giver.

Delio. You instruct me well.
Ant. Why, here's a man now would fright impudence
From sauciest beggars.
Pes. Prince Ferdinand's come to Milan,
Sick, as they give out, of an apoplexy;
But some say 'tis a frenzy: I am going
To visit him. [*Exit.*
Ant. 'Tis a noble old fellow.
Delio. What course do you mean to take, Antonio?
Ant. This night I mean to venture all my fortune,
Which is no more than a poor lingering life,
To the cardinal's worst of malice: I have got
Private access to his chamber; and intend
To visit him about the mid of night,
As once his brother did our noble duchess.
It may be that the sudden apprehension
Of danger,—for I'll go in mine own shape,—
When he shall see it fraight with love and duty,
May draw the poison out of him, and work
A friendly reconcilement: if it fail,
Yet it shall rid me of this imfamous calling;
For better fall once than be ever falling.
Delio. I'll second you in all danger; and howe'er,
My life keeps rank with yours.
Ant. You are still my lov'd and best friend. [*Exeunt.*

SCENE II

A gallery in the residence of the Cardinal and Ferdinand.

Enter Pescara and Doctor.

Pes. Now, doctor, may I visit your patient?
Doc. If 't please your lordship: but he's instantly
To take the air here in the gallery
By my direction.
Pes. Pray thee, what's his disease?
Doc. A very pestilent disease, my lord,
They call lycanthropia.
Pes. What's that?
I need a dictionary to 't.
Doc. I'll tell you.
In those that are possess'd with 't there o'erflows
Such melancholy humour they imagine
Themselves to be transformèd into wolves;
Steal forth to church-yards in the dead of night,
And dig dead bodies up: as two nights since
One met the duke 'bout midnight in a lane
Behind Saint Mark's church, with the leg of a man
Upon his shoulder; and he howl'd fearfully;
Said he was a wolf, only the difference
Was, a wolf's skin was hairy on the outside,
His on the inside; bade them take their swords,

Rip up his flesh, and try: straight I was sent for,
And, having minister'd to him, found his grace
Very well recover'd.

Pes. I am glad on 't.

Doc. Yet not without some fear
Of a relapse. If he grow to his fit again,
I'll go a nearer way to work with him
Than ever Paracelsus dream'd of; if
They'll give me leave, I'll buffet his madness out of him.
Stand aside; he comes.

Enter Ferdinand, Cardinal, Malatesti, and Bosola.

Ferd. Leave me.

Mal. Why doth your lordship love this solitariness?

Ferd. Eagles commonly fly alone: they are crows, daws, and starlings that flock together. Look, what's that follows me?

Mal. Nothing, my lord.

Ferd. Yes.

Mal. 'Tis your shadow.

Ferd. Stay it; let it not haunt me.

Mal. Impossible, if you move, and the sun shine.

Ferd. I will throttle it.

[*Throws himself down on his shadow.*

Mal. O, my lord, you are angry with nothing.

Ferd. You are a fool: how is't possible I should catch my shadow, unless I fall upon 't? When I go to hell,

I mean to carry a bribe; for, look you, good gifts evermore make way for the worst persons.

Pes. Rise, good my lord.

Ferd. I am studying the art of patience.

Pes. 'Tis a noble virtue.

Ferd. To drive six snails before me from this town to Moscow; neither use goad nor whip to them, but let them take their own time;—the patient'st man i' the world match me for an experiment:—and I'll crawl after like a sheep-biter.

Card. Force him up. [*They raise him.*

Ferd. Use me well, you were best. What I have done, I have done: I'll confess nothing.

Doc. Now let me come to him.—Are you mad, my lord? are you out of your princely wits?

Ferd. What's he?

Pes. Your doctor.

Ferd. Let me have his beard sawed off, and his eye-brows filed more civil.

Doc. I must do mad tricks with him, for that's the only way on't.—I have brought your grace a salamander's skin to keep you from sun-burning.

Ferd. I have cruel sore eyes.

Doc. The white of a cockatrix's egg is present remedy.

Ferd. Let it be a new-laid one, you were best.
Hide me from him: physicians are like kings,—
They brook no contradiction.

Doc. Now he begins to fear me: now let me alone with him.

Card. How now! put off your gown!

Doc. Let me have some forty urinals filled with rose-water: he and I'll go pelt one another with them. —Now he begins to fear me.—Can you fetch a frisk, sir?—Let him go, let him go, upon my peril: I find by his eye he stands in awe of me; I'll make him as tame as a dormouse.

Ferd. Can you fetch your frisks, sir!—I will stamp him into a cullis, flay off his skin, to cover one of the anatomies this rogue hath set i' the cold yonder in Barber-Chirurgeon's-hall.—Hence, hence! you are all of you like beasts for sacrifice: there's nothing left of you but tongue and belly, flattery and lechery. [*Exit.*

Pes. Doctor, he did not fear you throughly.

Doc. True; I was somewhat too forward.

Bos. Mercy upon me, what a fatal judgment
Hath fall'n upon this Ferdinand!

Pes. Knows your grace
What accident hath brought unto the prince
This strange distraction?

Card. [*aside.*] I must feign somewhat.—Thus they say it grew.
You have heard it rumour'd, for these many years
None of our family dies but there is seen
The shape of an old woman, which is given
By tradition to us to have been murder'd
By her nephews for her riches. Such a figure

One night, as the prince sat up late at 's book,
Appear'd to him; when crying out for help,
The gentleman of 's chamber found his grace
All on a cold sweat, alter'd much in face
And language: since which apparition,
He hath grown worse and worse, and I much fear
He cannot live.

Bos. Sir, I would speak with you.

Pes. We 'll leave your grace,
Wishing to the sick prince, our noble lord,
All health of mind and body.

Card. You are most welcome.

[*Exeunt Pescara, Malatesti, and Doctor.*

Are you come? so.—[*Aside.*] This fellow must not know
By any means I had intelligence
In our duchess' death; for, though I counsell'd it,
The full of all the engagement seem'd to grow
From Ferdinand.—Now, sir, how fares our sister?
I do not think but sorrow makes her look
Like to an oft-dy'd garment: she shall now
Take comfort from me. Why do you look so wildly?
O, the fortune of your master here the prince
Dejects you; but be you of happy comfort:
If you'll do one thing for me I 'll entreat,
Though he had a cold tomb-stone o'er his bones,
I 'd make you what you would be.

Bos. Any thing;

Give it me in a breath, and let me fly to 't:
They that think long small expedition win,
For musing much o' the end cannot begin.

Enter Julia.

Julia. Sir, will you come in to supper?
Card. I am busy; leave me.
Julia [*aside.*] What an excellent shape hath that fellow!
[*Exit.*
Card. 'Tis thus. Antonio lurks here in Milan:
Inquire him out, and kill him. While he lives,
Our sister cannot marry; and I have thought
Of an excellent match for her. Do this, and style me
Thy advancement.
Bos. But by what means shall I find him out?
Card. There is a gentleman call'd Delio
Here in the camp, that hath been long approv'd
His loyal friend. Set eye upon that fellow;
Follow him to mass; may be Antonio,
Although he do account religion
But a school-name, for fashion of the world
May accompany him; or else go inquire out
Delio's confessor, and see if you can bribe
Him to reveal it. There are a thousand ways
A man might find to trace him; as to know
What fellows haunt the Jews for taking up
Great sums of money, for sure he's in want;

Or else to go to the picture-makers, and learn
Who bought her picture lately: some of these
Happily may take.

Bos. Well, I 'll not freeze i' the business:
I would see that wretched thing, Antonio,
Above all sights i' the world.

Card. Do, and be happy. [*Exit.*

Bos. This fellow doth breed basilisks in 's eyes,
He 's nothing else but murder; yet he seems
Not to have notice of the duchess' death.
'Tis his cunning: I must follow his example;
There cannot be a surer way to trace
Than that of an old fox.

Re-enter Julia.

Julia. So, sir, you are well met.

Bos. How now!

Julia. Nay, the doors are fast enough:
Now, sir, I will make you confess your treachery.

Bos. Treachery!

Julia. Yes, confess to me
Which of my women 'twas you hir'd to put
Love-powder into my drink?

Bos. Love-powder!

Julia. Yes, when I was at Malfi.
Why should I fall in love with such a face else?
I have already suffer'd for thee so much pain,

The only remedy to do me good
Is to kill my longing.

Bos. Sure, your pistol holds
Nothing but perfumes or kissing-comfits.
Excellent lady!
You have a pretty way on't to discover
Your longing. Come, come, I'll disarm you,
And arm you thus: yet this is wondrous strange.

Julia. Compare thy form and my eyes together,
You'll find my love no such great miracle.
Now you'll say
I am wanton: this nice modesty in ladies
Is but a troublesome familiar
That haunts them.

Bos. Know you me, I am a blunt soldier.

Julia. The better:
Sure, there wants fire where there are no lively sparks
Of roughness.

Bos. And I want compliment.

Julia. Why, ignorance
In courtship cannot make you do amiss,
If you have a heart to do well.

Bos. You are very fair.

Julia. Nay, if you lay beauty to my charge,
I must plead unguilty.

Bos. Your bright eyes
Carry a quiver of darts in them sharper
Than sun-beams.

Julia. You will mar me with commendation,
Put yourself to the charge of courting me,
Whereas now I woo you.
Bos. [*aside.*] I have it, I will work upon this creature.—
Let us grow most amorously familiar:
If the great cardinal now should see me thus,
Would he not count me a villain?
Julia. No; he might count me a wanton,
Not lay a scruple of offence on you;
For if I see and steal a diamond,
The fault is not i' the stone, but in me the thief
That purloins it. I am sudden with you:
We that are great women of pleasure use to cut off
These uncertain wishes and unquiet longings,
And in an instant join the sweet delight
And the pretty excuse together. Had you been i' the street,
Under my chamber-window, even there
I should have courted you.
Bos. O, you are an excellent lady!
Julia. Bid me do somewhat for you presently
To express I love you.
Bos. I will; and if you love me,
Fail not to effect it.
The cardinal is grown wondrous melancholy;
Demand the cause, let him not put you off
With feign'd excuse; discover the main ground on't.
Julia. Why would you know this?

Bos. I have depended on him,
And I hear that he is fall'n in some disgrace
With the emperor: if he be, like the mice
That forsake falling houses, I would shift
To other dependance.

Julia. You shall not need
Follow the wars: I'll be your maintenance.

Bos. And I your loyal servant: but I cannot
Leave my calling.

Julia. Not leave an ungrateful
General for the love of a sweet lady!
You are like some cannot sleep in feather-beds,
But must have blocks for their pillows.

Bos. Will you do this?

Julia. Cunningly.

Bos. To-morrow I'll expect the intelligence.

Julia. To-morrow! get you into my cabinet;
You shall have it with you. Do not delay me,
No more than I do you: I am like one
That is condemn'd; I have my pardon promis'd,
But I would see it seal'd. Go, get you in:
You shall see me wind my tongue about his heart
Like a skein of silk. [*Exit Bosola.*

Re-enter Cardinal.

Card. Where are you?

Enter Servants.

Servants. Here.

Card. Let none, upon your lives, have conference
With the Prince Ferdinand, unless I know it.—
[*Aside*] In this distraction he may reveal
The murder. [*Exeunt Servants.*
Yond 's my lingering consumption:
I am weary of her, and by any means
Would be quit of.

Julia. How now, my lord! what ails you?

Card. Nothing.

Julia. O, you are much alter'd:
Come, I must be your secretary, and remove
This lead from off your bosom: what 's the matter?

Card. I may not tell you.

Julia. Are you so far in love with sorrow
You cannot part with part of it? or think you
I cannot love your grace when you are sad
As well as merry? or do you suspect
I, that have a been a secret to your heart
These many winters, cannot be the same
Unto your tongue?

Card. Satisfy thy longing,—
The only way to make thee keep my counsel
Is, not to tell thee.

Julia. Tell your echo this,
Or flatterers, that like echoes still report

What they hear though most imperfect, and not me;
For if that you be true unto yourself,
I'll know.

Card. Will you rack me?

Julia. No, judgment shall
Draw it from you: it is an equal fault,
To tell one's secrets unto all or none.

Card. The first argues folly.

Julia. But the last tyranny.

Card. Very well: why, imagine I have committed
Some secret deed which I desire the world
May never hear of.

Julia. Therefore may not I know it?
You have conceal'd for me as great a sin
As adultery. Sir, never was occasion
For perfect trial of my constancy
Till now: sir, I beseech you——

Card. You'll repent it.

Julia. Never.

Card. It hurries thee to ruin: I'll not tell thee.
Be well advis'd, and think what danger 'tis
To receive a prince's secrets: they that do,
Had need have their breasts hoop'd with adamant
To contain them. I pray thee, yet be satisfied;
Examine thine own frailty; 'tis more easy
To tie knots than unloose them: 'tis a secret
That, like a lingering poison, may chance lie
Spread in thy veins, and kill thee seven year hence.

Julia. Now you dally with me.

Card. No more; thou shalt know it.
By my appointment the great Duchess of Malfi
And two of her young children, four nights since,
Were strangl'd.

Julia. O heaven! sir, what have you done!

Card. How now? how settles this? think you your bosom
Will be a grave dark and obscure enough
For such a secret?

Julia. You have undone yourself, sir.

Card. Why?

Julia. It lies not in me to conceal it.

Card. No?
Come, I will swear you to 't upon this book.

Julia. Most religiously.

Card. Kiss it. [*She kisses the book.*
Now you shall never utter it; thy curiosity
Hath undone thee: thou 'rt poison'd with that book;
Because I knew thou couldst not keep my counsel,
I have bound thee to 't by death.

Re-enter Bosola.

Bos. For pity-sake, hold!

Card. Ha, Bosola!

Julia. I forgive you
This equal piece of justice you have done;
For I betray'd your counsel to that fellow:

He over-heard it; that was the cause I said
It lay not in me to conceal it.
Bos. O foolish woman,
Couldst thou not have poison'd him?
Julia. 'Tis weakness,
Too much to think what should have been done. I go,
I know not whither. [*Dies.*
Card. Wherefore com'st thou hither?
Bos. That I might find a great man like yourself,
Not out of his wits as the Lord Ferdinand,
To remember my service.
Card. I'll have thee hew'd in pieces.
Bos. Make not yourself such a promise of that life
Which is not yours to dispose of.
Card. Who plac'd thee here?
Bos. Her lust, as she intended.
Card. Very well:
Now you know me for your fellow-murderer.
Bos. And wherefore should you lay fair marble colours
Upon your rotten purposes to me?
Unless you imitate some that do plot great treasons,
And when they have done, go hide themselves i' the grave
Of those were actors in 't?
Card. No more; there is
A fortune attends thee.
Bos. Shall I go sue to Fortune any longer?
'Tis the fool's pilgrimage.

Card. I have honours in store for thee.

Bos. There are many ways that conduct to seeming honour,
And some of them very dirty ones.

Card. Throw to the devil
Thy melancholy. The fire burns well;
What need we keep a stirring of 't, and make
A greater smother? Thou wilt kill Antonio?

Bos. Yes.

Card. Take up that body.

Bos. I think I shall
Shortly grow the common bier for church-yards.

Card. I will allow thee some dozen of attendants
To aid thee in the murder.

Bos. O, by no means. Physicians that apply horse-leeches to any rank swelling use to cut off their tails, that the blood may run through them the faster: let me have no train when I go to shed blood, lest it make me have a greater when I ride to the gallows.

Card. Come to me after midnight, to help to remove
That body to her own lodging: I'll give out
She died o' the plague; 'twill breed the less inquiry
After her death.

Bos. Where's Castruccio her husband?

Card. He's rode to Naples, to take possession
Of Antonio's citadel.

Bos. Believe me, you have done a very happy turn.

Card. Fail not to come: there is the master-key

Of our lodgings; and by that you may conceive
What trust I plant in you.

Bos. You shall find me ready. [*Exit Cardinal.*
O poor Antonio, though nothing be so needful
To thy estate as pity, yet I find
Nothing so dangerous! I must look to my footing:
In such slippery ice-pavements men had need
To be frost-nail'd well, they may break their necks else;
The precedent's here afore me. How this man
Bears up in blood! seems fearless! Why, 'tis well;
Security some men call the suburbs of hell,
Only a dead wall between. Well, good Antonio,
I'll seek thee out; and all my care shall be
To put thee into safety from the reach
Of these most cruel biters that have got
Some of thy blood already. It may be,
I'll join with thee in a most just revenge:
The weakest arm is strong enough that strikes
With the sword of justice. Still methinks the duchess
Haunts me: there, there!—'Tis nothing but my melancholy.
O Penitence, let me truly taste thy cup,
That throws men down only to raise them up!
[*Exit.*

SCENE III

A Fortification.

Enter Antonio and Delio.

Delio. Yond 's the cardinal's window. This fortification
Grew from the ruins of an ancient abbey ;
And to yond side o' the river lies a wall,
Piece of a cloister, which in my opinion
Gives the best echo that you ever heard,
So hollow and so dismal, and withal
So plain in the distinction of our words,
That many have suppos'd it is a spirit
That answers.
Ant. I do love these ancient ruins.
We never tread upon them but we set
Our foot upon some reverend history :
And, questionless, here in this open court,
Which now lies naked to the injuries
Of stormy weather, some men lie interr'd
Lov'd the church so well, and gave so largely to 't,
They thought it should have canopied their bones
Till dooms-day ; but all things have their end :
Churches and cities, which have diseases like to men,
Must have like death that we have.
Echo. Like death that we have.

Delio. Now the echo hath caught you.
Ant. It groan'd methought, and gave
A very deadly accent.
Echo. Deadly accent.
Delio. I told you 'twas a pretty one : you may make it
A huntsman, or a falconer, a musician,
Or a thing of sorrow.
Echo. A thing of sorrow.
Ant. Ay, sure, that suits it best.
Echo. That suits it best.
Ant. 'Tis very like my wife's voice.
Echo. Ay, wife's voice.
Delio. Come, let us walk further from 't.
I would not have you go to the cardinal's to-night :
Do not.
Echo. Do not.
Delio. Wisdom doth not more moderate wasting sorrow
Than time : take time for 't ; be mindful of thy safety.
Echo. Be mindful of thy safety.
Ant. Necessity compels me :
Make scrutiny through the passages
Of your own life, you'll find it impossible
To fly your fate.
Echo. O, fly your fate!
Delio. Hark! the dead stones seem to have pity on you,
And give you good counsel.

Ant. Echo, I will not talk with thee,
For thou art a dead thing.
Echo. Thou art a dead thing.
Ant. My duchess is asleep now,
And her little ones, I hope sweetly: O heaven,
Shall I never see her more?
Echo. Never see her more.
Ant. I mark'd not one repetition of the echo
But that; and on the sudden a clear light
Presented me a face folded in sorrow.
Delio. Your fancy merely.
Ant. Come, I'll be out of this ague,
For to live thus is not indeed to live;
It is a mockery and abuse of life:
I will not henceforth save myself by halves;
Lose all, or nothing.
Delio. Your own virtue save you!
I'll fetch your eldest son, and second you:
It may be that the sight of his own blood
Spread in so sweet a figure may beget
The more compassion. However, fare you well.
Though in our miseries Fortune have a part,
Yet in our noble sufferings she hath none:
Contempt of pain, that we may call our own.
[*Exeunt.*

SCENE IV

An apartment in the residence of the Cardinal and Ferdinand.

Enter Cardinal, Pescara, Malatesti, Roderigo, and Grisolan.

Card. You shall not watch to-night by the sick prince;
His grace is very well recover'd.
Mal. Good my lord, suffer us.
Card. O, by no means;
The noise, and change of object in his eye,
Doth more distract him: I pray, all to bed;
And though you hear him in his violent fit,
Do not rise, I entreat you.
Pes. So, sir; we shall not.
Card. Nay, I must have you promise
Upon your honours, for I was enjoin'd to 't
By himself; and he seem'd to urge it sensibly.
Pes. Let our honours bind this trifle.
Card. Nor any of your followers.
Mal. Neither.
Card. It may be, to make trial of your promise,
When he 's asleep, myself will rise and feign
Some of his mad tricks, and cry out for help,
And feign myself in danger.
Mal. If your throat were cutting,
I 'd not come at you, now I have protested against it.

Card. Why, I thank you.
[*Withdraws to the upper end of the apartment.*
Gris. 'Twas a foul storm to-night.
Rod. The Lord Ferdinand's chamber shook like an osier.
Mal. 'Twas nothing but pure kindness in the devil
To rock his own child.
[*Exeunt all except the Cardinal.*
Card. The reason why I would not suffer these
About my brother, is, because at midnight
I may with better privacy convey
Julia's body to her own lodging. O, my conscience!
I would pray now; but the devil takes away my heart 31
For having any confidence in prayer.
About this hour I appointed Bosola
To fetch the body: when he hath serv'd my turn,
He dies. [*Exit.*

Enter Bosola.

Bos. Ha! 'twas the cardinal's voice; I heard him name
Bosola and my death. Listen; I hear one's footing.

Enter Ferdinand.

Ferd. Strangling is a very quiet death.
Bos. [*aside.*] Nay, then, I see I must stand upon my guard.
Ferd. What say [you] to that? whisper softly; do you

agree to't? So; it must be done i' the dark: the cardinal would not for a thousand pounds the doctor should see it. [*Exit.*

Bos. My death is plotted; here's the consequence of murder.
We value not desert nor Christian breath,
When we know black deeds must be cur'd with death.

Enter Antonio and Servant.

Serv. Here stay, sir, and be confident, I pray:
I'll fetch you a dark lantern. [*Exit.*

Ant. Could I take him at his prayers,
There were hope of pardon.

Bos. Fall right, my sword!— [*Stabs him.*
I'll not give thee so much leisure as to pray.

Ant. O, I am gone! Thou hast ended a long suit
In a minute.

Bos. What art thou?

Ant. A most wretched thing,
That only have thy benefit in death,
To appear myself.

Re-enter Servant with a lantern.

Serv. Where are you, sir?

Ant. Very near my home.—Bosola!

Serv. O, misfortune!

Bos. Smother thy pity, thou art dead else.—Antonio !
The man I would have sav'd 'bove mine own life !
We are merely the stars' tennis-balls, struck and banded
Which way please them.—O good Antonio,
I 'll whisper one thing in thy dying ear
Shall make thy heart break quickly ! thy fair duchess
And two sweet children——

Ant. Their very names
Kindle a little life in me.

Bos. Are murder'd.

Ant. Some men have wish'd to die
At the hearing of sad tidings ; I am glad
That I shall do 't in sadness : I would not now
Wish my wounds balm'd nor heal'd, for I have no use
To put my life to. In all our quest of greatness,
Like wanton boys whose pastime is their care,
We follow after bubbles blown in the air.
Pleasure of life, what is 't ? only the good hours
Of an ague ; merely a preparative to rest,
To endure vexation. I do not ask
The process of my death ; only commend me
To Delio.

Bos. Break, heart !

Ant. And let my son fly the courts of princes. [*Dies.*

Bos. Thou seem'st to have lov'd Antonio.

Serv. I brought him hither,
To have reconcil'd him to the cardinal.
Bos. I do not ask thee that.
Take him up, if thou tender thine own life,
And bear him where the lady Julia
Was wont to lodge.—O, my fate moves swift!
I have this cardinal in the forge already;
Now I'll bring him to the hammer. O direful misprision!
I will not imitate things glorious,
No more than base; I'll be mine own example.—
On, on, and look thou represent, for silence,
The thing thou bar'st. [*Exeunt.*

SCENE V

Another apartment in the same.

Enter Cardinal, with a book.

Card. I am puzzled in a question about hell;
He says, in hell there's one material fire,
And yet it shall not burn all men alike.
Lay him by. How tedious is a guilty conscience!
When I look into the fish-ponds in my garden,
Methinks I see a thing arm'd with a rake,
That seems to strike at me.

Enter Bosola, and Servant bearing Antonio's body.

Now, art thou come?
Thou look'st ghastly:
There sits in thy face some great determination
Mix'd with some fear.

Bos. Thus it lightens into action:
I am come to kill thee.

Card. Ha!—Help! our guard!

Bos. Thou art deceiv'd;
They are out of thy howling.

Card. Hold; and I will faithfully divide
Revenues with thee.

Bos. Thy prayers and proffers
Are both unseasonable.

Card. Raise the watch! we are betray'd!

Bos. I have confin'd your flight:
I'll suffer your retreat to Julia's chamber,
But no further.

Card. Help! we are betray'd!

Enter, above, Pescara, Malatesti, Roderigo, and Grisolan.

Mal. Listen.

Card. My dukedom for rescue!

Rod. Fie upon his counterfeiting!

Mal. Why, 'tis not the cardinal.

Rod. Yes, yes, 'tis he:
But, I'll see him hang'd ere I'll go down to him.

Card. Here 's a plot upon me ; I am assaulted ! I am lost,
Unless some rescue !
Gris. He doth this pretty well ;
But it will not serve to laugh me out of mine honour.
Card. The sword 's at my throat !
Rod. You would not bawl so loud then.
Mal. Come, come, let 's go
To bed : he told us this much aforehand.
Pes. He wish'd you should not come at him ; but, believe 't,
The accent of the voice sounds not in jest :
I 'll down to him, howsoever, and with engines
Force ope the doors. [*Exit above.*
Rod. Let 's follow him aloof,
And note how the cardinal will laugh at him.
[*Exeunt, above, Malatesti, Roderigo, and Grisolan.*
Bos. There 's for you first,
'Cause you shall not unbarricade the door
To let in rescue. [*Kills the Servant.*
Card. What cause hast thou to pursue my life ?
Bos. Look there.
Card. Antonio !
Bos. Slain by my hand unwittingly.
Pray, and be sudden : when thou kill'd'st thy sister,
Thou took'st from Justice her most equal balance,
And left her naught but her sword.

Card. O, mercy!
Bos. Now it seems thy greatness was only outward;
For thou fall'st faster of thyself than calamity
Can drive thee. I'll not waste longer time; there!
[*Stabs him.*
Card. Thou hast hurt me.
Bos. Again! [*Stabs him again.*
Card. Shall I die like a leveret,
Without any resistance?—Help, help, help!
I am slain!

Enter Ferdinand.

Ferd. The alarum! give me a fresh horse;
Rally the vaunt-guard, or the day is lost,
Yield, yield! I give you the honour of arms
Shake my sword over you; will you yield?
Card. Help me; I am your brother!
Ferd. The devil!
My brother fight upon the adverse party!
[*He wounds the Cardinal, and, in the scuffle, gives Bosola his death-wound.*
There flies your ransom.
Card. O justice!
I suffer now for what hath former bin:
Sorrow is held the eldest child of sin.
Ferd. Now you're brave fellows. Cæsar's fortune was harder than Pompey's; Cæsar died in the arms of prosperity, Pompey at the feet of disgrace. You

both died in the field. The pain 's nothing : pain many times is taken away with the apprehension of greater, as the tooth-ache with the sight of a barber that comes to pull it out : there 's philosophy for you.

Bos. Now my revenge is perfect.—Sink, thou main cause
[*Kills Ferdinand.*
Of my undoing !—The last part of my life
Hath done me best service.

Ferd. Give me some wet hay ; I am broken-winded.
I do account this world but a dog-kennel :
I will vault credit and affect high pleasures
Beyond death.

Bos. He seems to come to himself,
Now he's so near the bottom.

Ferd. My sister, O my sister ! there 's the cause on 't.
Whether we fall by ambition, blood, or lust,
Like diamonds, we are cut with our own dust.
[*Dies.*

Card. Thou hast thy payment too.

Bos. Yes, I hold my weary soul in my teeth ;
'Tis ready to part from me. I do glory
That thou, which stood'st like a huge pyramid
Begun upon a large and ample base,
Shalt end in a little point, a kind of nothing.

Enter, below, Pescara, Malatesti, Roderigo, and Grisolan.

Pes. How now, my lord!
Mal. O sad disaster!
Rod. How comes this?
Bos. Revenge for the Duchess of Malfi murder'd
By the Arragonian brethren; for Antonio
Slain by this hand; for lustful Julia
Poison'd by this man; and lastly for myself,
That was an actor in the main of all
Much 'gainst mine own good nature, yet i' the end
Neglected.
Pes. How now, my lord!
Card. Look to my brother:
He gave us these large wounds, as we were struggling
Here i' the rushes. And now, I pray, let me
Be laid by and never thought of. [*Dies.*
Pes. How fatally, it seems, he did withstand
His own rescue!
Mal. Thou wretched thing of blood,
How came Antonio by his death?
Bos. In a mist; I know not how:
Such a mistake as I have often seen
In a play. O, I am gone!
We are only like dead walls or vaulted graves,
That, ruin'd, yield no echo. Fare you well.
It may be pain, but no harm, to me to die

In so good a quarrel. O, this gloomy world!
In what a shadow, or deep pit of darkness,
Doth womanish and fearful mankind live!
Let worthy minds ne'er stagger in distrust
To suffer death or shame for what is just:
Mine is another voyage. [*Dies.*

Pes. The noble Delio, as I came to the palace,
Told me of Antonio's being here, and show'd me
A pretty gentleman, his son and heir.

Enter Delio, and Antonio's Son.

Mal. O sir, you come too late!

Delio. I heard so, and
Was arm'd for 't, ere I came. Let us make noble use
Of this great ruin; and join all our force
To establish this young hopeful gentleman
In 's mother's right. These wretched eminent things
Leave no more fame behind 'em, than should one
Fall in a frost, and leave his print in snow;
As soon as the sun shines, it ever melts,
Both form and matter. I have ever thought
Nature doth nothing so great for great men
As when she 's pleas'd to make them lords of truth:
Integrity of life is fame's best friend,
Which nobly, beyond death, shall crown the end.

[*Exeunt.*

GLOSSARY

ANGEL, the coin of that name, with a reference also to the common sense of the word. Act I. Sc. i.

APPROVE, to experience. Act II. Sc. iv.

ARRAS, white powder. Act. III. Sc.ii. So 'Her hair is sprinkled with arras powder
That makes her look as if she had sinned in the pastry.'
Vittoria Corombona.

ATONEMENT, reconciliation. Act IV. Sc. ii.

BLACK-GUARD, the meanest drudges in a great household. Act II. Sc. ii. So 'A lousy slave that rode with the black-guard in the duke's carriage, 'mongst spits and dripping pans.'—*Vittoria Corombona.* Hence our modern term of abuse.

CAREEN, to lay a ship on its side for repairs. Act II. Sc. i.

CENSURE, judgment. Act III. Sc. i. So 'Take each man's censure but reserve thy judgment.'—*Hamlet*, I. iii. 69.

CHARGEABLE, extravagant. Act. I. Sc. i.

CHEAT, escheat, *i.e.* the falling of a fief to the feudal lord. Here *in cheat* means *in fee*. Act V. Sc. ii.

COMPLIMENTAL, ornamental. Act I. Sc. i. There is a kindred sense of *Compliment* (for 'Accomplishment') in *Love's Labour Lost*, I. i. 169.

CONSORT, concert. Act IV. Sc. ii.

CULLIS, strong broth. Act II. Sc. iv., Sc. v., Act V. Sc. ii.

DISEMBOGUE, to discharge; properly of a river into the sea, here of a leaky ship in dock. Act II. Sc. i.

ENGINOUS, of machinery, *i.e.* swift. Act III. Sc. ii. So *Engine* in the same scene.

FOOT-CLOTH, the housing of a horse. Act II. Sc. i.

FRAIGHT, fraught. Act V. Sc. I.

GALLIARD, a quick dance. Act I. Sc. i. So *Twelfth Night*, I. iii. 137. The word is taken either from Spanish or Italian.

GORDIAN, knot. Act I. Sc. i.

GUARDED, embroidered, faced. Act III. Sc. iii.

HUSBAND, householder or economist. Act I. Sc. i. So *Husbandry*, *Macbeth*, II. i. 5; *Hamlet*, I. iii. 77.

IMPOSTHUME, ulcer. Act IV. Sc. ii. So 'This is the imposthume of much wealth and peace.'—*Hamlet*, IV. iii. 27.

INGENIOUS, ingenuous. Act I. Sc. i. So 'I do wish ingeniously for thy sake
The dog-days all year long.'
Vittoria Corombona.

INTELLIGENCE, (1) spying (?), Act IV. Sc. i.; (2) Complicity, Act V. Sc. ii. This may be the sense also in the former passage.

INTELLIGENCER, spy. Act I. Sc. i., Act III. Sc. ii. Compare the sense of 'Intelligence' in the same scene and in Act II. Sc. iii.

LEAGUER, camp. Act I. Sc. i., Act III. Sc. iii.

LIBEL, to write, engross. Act II. Sc. iii.

LUXURIOUS, wanton. Act I. Sc. i. Cf. *Merry Wives of Windsor*, V. v. 98.

MISRULE, Lord of; a reference to the office of Master at the Christmastide Revels. Act III. Sc. ii. See the accounts quoted in Collier's *Annals of the Stage*, i. 44-50 (Henry VII.).

MISPRISION, mistake. Act V. Sc. iv.

MORPHEW, scab, ulcer. Act II. Sc. i.

MOTION, (1) resolve, Act I. Sc. i. An almost identical use (for 'Will') is found in *Othello*, I. ii. 75. (2) Picture, image, Act III. Sc. ii. See the note.

MOTHER, hysterics. Act II. Sc. i. So *Lear*, II. iv. 56.

MUMMY, a substance supposed to be distilled from mummies and used as medicine. Act IV. Sc. ii.

NIGHT-CAP, apparently used of lawyers. Act II. Sc. i. It is so used again in *The Devil's Law-Case*, II. i.—'Among a shoal or swarm of reeking night-caps.'

OWE, own. Act IV. Sc. i. So 'Nor lose possession of that fair thou owest.'—Shakespeare, *Sonnet* 18.

PERSPECTIVE, glass, telescope. Act IV. Sc. ii.

PEWTERER, worker in pewter. Act III. Sc. iii. So 2 *Henry IV.*, III. ii. 281.

PHYSICAL, medicinal. Act II. Sc. iv. It is used in a kindred sense—'healthy'—in *Julius Cæsar*, II. i. 261.

PROGRESS, a royal progress. Act II. Sc. i.

PURCHASE, riches, gains. Act III. Sc. i. So 'His purchase was greater than his rent.'—Chaucer, *Prologue*.

QUESTION, investigation, inquisition. Act II. Sc. iii.

QUIETUS EST, the formula used in giving a quittance of accounts. Act I. Sc. i., Act III. Sc. ii.

RADICAL, searching. Act II. Sc. iii.

ROARING BOY, swaggerer, swashbuckler. Act II. Sc. i. Hence the title of the famous play by Middleton and Dekker, *The Roaring Girl*. *Angry Boy*, as in Jonson's *Alchemist*, meant the same thing.

RUPTURE, outburst. Act II. Sc. iv. Dyce suggests *rapture*, but this is not necessary.

SADNESS, earnest. Act V. Sc. iv.

SALVATORY, ointment-box. Act IV. Sc. ii.

SHEEP-BITER, thief. Act V. Sc. ii. So *Twelfth Night*, II. v. 6.

SHREWD TURN, ill turn. Act I. Sc. I. Cf. *Henry VIII.*, V. iii. 178.

SIMPLICITY, folly. Act II. Sc. i. So 'Simple truth miscalled simplicity.'—Shakespeare, *Sonnet* 66.

SLEDGE, sledge-hammer. Act II. Sc. v.

SMOTHER, dense stifling smoke. Act V. Sc. ii. So 'Thus must I from the smoke into the smother.' —*As You Like It*, I. ii. 229.

SPRINGAL, shoot, infant. Act II. Sc. i.

TENT, a play on the medical sense of the word *tent*, *i.e.* the material, lint or other, used in probing a wound. The verb 'tent' means to probe, as in 'The untented woundings of a father's curse.'—*Lear*, I. iv. 322.

TETCHINESS, crossness. Act II. Sc. i. So 'Tetchy and wayward was thy infancy.'—*Richard III.*, IV. iv. 168.

TETTER, scab or scurf. Act II. Sc. i. So *Hamlet*, I. v. 71.

TRANSPORTATION, exportation. Act IV. Sc. ii.

TRAVERSE, side-scene, curtain. Act IV. Sc. i.

UNVALUED, invaluable. Act III. Sc. ii. So 'Inestimable stones, unvalued jewels.'—*Richard III.*, I. iv. 27.

WHEN? an exclamation of impatience. Act II. Sc. i.

WOLF, cancer, lupus. Act II. Sc. i.

NOTES

I. i. 1. In the two opening speeches there is plainly a historical allusion; and probably to contemporary events. I incline to think that the reference may be to the assassination of Concini, Maréchal d'Ancre, by order of the young king, Louis XIII. Concini, the favourite of the queen-mother, was bitterly hated; and his murder was skilfully represented as an act of justice against a public enemy and a traitor. Luines, who advised the king in the matter and succeeded to the power of Concini, made a parade of calling the old councillors of Henry IV.—'les vieux serviteurs du feu roi son père'—back to court. (See Martin, *Histoire de France*, t. xi. pp. 112 121.)

If this suggestion be well founded—but it is offered with great diffidence—we should be able to fix the date of the Play more closely, to 1617-18. Concini was assassinated in April 1617; and, for the reason stated in the Preface, the Play must have been written by the end of the following year.

I. i. 10. *Which, i.e.* his palace.

I. i. 23. *What they ought to foresee.* A contrast seems to be intended between telling a prince what he ought to do and giving him such information as shall enable him to form his own judgment on the case.

I. i. 37. *I wore two towels*: like Falstaff's regiment, 1 *Henry IV.*, IV. ii. 48.

I. i. 41. *Dog-days.* Days of ill-luck, which the rising of the dog-star was supposed to signify. Browne, *Vulgar Errors*, iv. 13.

I. i. 61. *Nor ever died any man.* The Quarto reads '*did*,' but it is clearly a misprint. In the same sentence the Quarto reads 'he that hoped for a *pleadon.*' Possibly this is a misprint for '*pleader*, but more probably for '*pardon.*'

I. i. 75. With Delio's speech the Quarto begins a new scene; wrongly, according to modern custom.

I. l. 95. *Who took the Ring?* An allusion to the sport of tilting at the ring.

I. i. 128. Pliny, *Hist. Nat.*, viii. 67 (Dyce). The fable was specially applied to Spanish horses, as we learn from Pliny, and from Browne, *Vulgar Errors*, III. iii.

I. i. 133. *Laugh but when I laugh.* The Quarto omits '*but*, which is necessary to the sense.

I. i. 224. *She stains the time past, etc.* This line occurs again in Webster's *Monumental Column*, about fifty lines from the end. Webster is apt to repeat himself. Thus the lines—

> 'I have seen children oft eat sweetmeats thus
> As fearful to devour them too soon'—

occur both in this scene towards the close, and in *Appius and Virginia*, I. i. See also Act IV. Sc. i. l. 44, and Sc. ii. l. 169.

I. i. 313. *Candies all sins o'er.* The Quarto misprints '*are.*' The phrase occurs again in *Northward Ho*, I. iii.—

> 'I'll candy o'er my words and sleek my brow.'

I. i. 404. *I winked and chose a husband*: *i.e.* either (1) chose with my eyes shut, or (2) chose in the twinkling of an eye.

I. i. 462. *'Twere stranger.* The Quarto reads '*strange*'; but both metre and sense require '*stranger.*'

I. i. 589. *Alexander and Ludowick.* Dyce quotes the title of the old ballad, here referred to: '*The two faithful friends*, the pleasant history of Alexander and Lodwicke, who were so like one another that none could know them asunder; wherein is declared how Lodwicke married the Princesse of Hungaria, in Alexander's name, and how each night he layd a naked Sword betweene him and the Princesse, because he would not wrong his friend.' The incident is common in mediæval romance; *e.g. Amis et Amiles*, l. 1156-1166.

II. i. 42. *Fat of serpents, etc.* As in the witches' caldron of *Macbeth*, IV. i.

II. i. 73. *Most teeming blue*: blue, like those of a woman with child.

II. i. 127. *Swoon.* The Quarto reads '*sound*.' The same popular form occurs in *The Ancient Mariner*—

'Like noises in a swound.'

II. ii. 88. *Throwing down salt, or crossing of a hare.* See Browne, *Vulgar Errors*, V. xxiii.

II. iii. 27. *I have been setting a figure For the duchess' jewels*: *i.e.* making an astrological calculation to discover who stole them. The phrase is used in the same sense at the close of the preceding scene; and the scientific terminology is kept up in the following '*question*' and '*radical*.'

II. iii. 54. *You libel well, sir.* Here Antonio hands the paper containing the calculation concerning the theft of the jewels to Bosola, and orders him to copy it. Bosola refuses, offering to sign it when copied by Antonio, and so braving the imputations that Antonio has cast on him. Antonio, in going out, drops another paper, containing the horoscope of the new-born infant. Bosola observes the mistake and takes the dark lantern—'Some of your help, false friend'—to look for the paper.

II. iv. 24. *That fantastic glass.* Galileo's famous telescope was first exhibited, at Venice, in 1609. Hallam, *Literary History*, III. 425.

II. iv. 107. *And deep woes do shun*: *i.e.* pass through whirlpools unharmed.

II. v. 1. *Digg'd up a mandrake.* It was a popular superstition that the shrieks of a mandrake brought death or madness. See Browne, *Vulgar Errors*, II. vi. So Shakespeare,

'Shrieks like mandrakes' torn out of the earth,
That living mortals, hearing them, run mad.
Romeo and Juliet, IV. iii. 47.

II. v. 44. *So far upon the left side*: supposed to be a sign of folly. 'A wise man's heart is at his right hand; but a fool's heart at his left'—*Ecclesiastes*, x. 2. See Browne, *Vulgar Errors*, IV. ii.

II. v. 103. *Fix her in a general eclipse.* I believe this means 'plunge her in darkness'; but it is not satisfactory.

III. i. 51. *He's a mere stick of sugar-candy.* The phrase occurs again with the same addition—'A man may look quite through you'—in *The Devil's Law-Case*, II. i.

III. i. 59. *One of Pasquil's paper bullets*: *i.e.* a Pasquinade.

III. i. 106. *Put a girdle 'bout the world.* Besides the well-known passage in *Midsummer Night's Dream*, this phrase is found also in Chapman's *Bussy d'Ambois*, I. i., and in Massinger's *Maid of Honour*, I. i., where it is used of England—

'The empress of the European isles.'

III. ii. 48. *A motion.* I think it probable that this means '*picture*' or '*image*,' almost the equivalent of the modern *Tableau vivant.* The use of '*motion*' for '*puppet*' is well known, being found in Milton's *Areopagitica*—'Such an Adam as he is in the motions.' And the word is found, either as an equivalent for '*picture*' or in close connection with it, in Jonson's *Alchemist*, V. i.:

'Sure he has got
Some bawdy pictures . . .
The friar and the nun; or the new motion
Of the knight's courser.'

There is a like passage in *Every Man Out of His Humour*, II. i. 5.

III. ii. 158. *You have shook hands with Reputation*: *i.e.* bade farewell to him. So: 'Yet I have not so shaken hands with those desperate resolutions . . . as to stand in diameter and sword's point with them.'—*Religio Medici*, § 3.

III. ii. 219. *Magnanima menzogna*: the phrase applied by Tasso to the heroic fraud of Sofronia, related in Canto II. of his Poem.

III. ii. 255. *A pig's head gaping.* Jews were supposed to take special offence at this sight. Hence the words—

'Some men there are love not a gaping pig'—

are peculiarly apt in the mouth of Shylock. *Merchant of Venice*, IV. i.

III. ii. 268. *Scour his gold chain*: the badge of stewardship. So Sir Toby to Malvolio: 'Go, sir, rub your chain with crumbs.' —*Twelfth Night*, II. iii. 128.

III. ii. 286. *Pluto, the god of riches*: a confusion with Plutus, not uncommon either in Greek or English literature. The following fable is given in Bacon's Essay *Of Riches.*

III. ii. 357. *Our Lady of Loretto.* In Painter and his original, Belleforest, this suggestion is made by Cariola; in Webster, with far truer effect it comes from Bosola, and draws a protest from Cariola. The following sentence from Belleforest, literally translated by Painter, is a fair sample of the way in which both writers handle the story: 'Il ne suffit point à ceste folle femme d'avoir pris mary plus pour rassasier sa lubricité que pour autre occasion, si à son pechè elle n'aioustoit une execrable impiété, faisant les saincts lieux et les offices de devotion estre comme les ministres de sa folie.' Ed. 1565, t. ii. p. 18.

III. iii. 8. *Taking the French king prisoner.* A reference to the defeat of Francis I. at Pavia (1525) by the imperial troops under Pescara, the Constable Bourbon, and Lannoy; it was to Lannoy that Francis yielded up his sword.

III. iii. 40. *A guarded sumpter-cloth*: *i.e.* not a war-horse, but only a horse-cloth, with fine facings, such as was used on occasions of ceremony.

III. iv. 8. 'The Author disclaimes this Ditty to be his' is the marginal note on these rhymes in the Quarto of 1623.

III. v. 82. *Thou art happy that thou hast not understanding.* The thought is the same as that of the farewell of Ajax to his son: Sophocles, *Ajax*, 552. But it is improbable that Webster had read the Greek dramatist.

III. v. 113. *Overcharg'd with princes.* This image is common in the poetry of the Middle Ages, the first suggestion of it apparently coming from Boethius (Book II., Prose 1, 2; Metre i.). There is a fine drawing in the Uffizi Gallery at Florence, representing the same thought to the eye.

III. v. 145. *Counterfeit face*, his vizard.

IV. i. 54. *For though our national law.* So in *The Devil's Law-Case*, IV. ii.—

> 'For though our civil law makes difference
> Between the base and the legitimate,
> Compassionate nature makes them equal.'

IV. i. 165. *By my intelligence*: *i.e.* by my having acted as spy.

IV. ii. 65. *An excellent knave in grain.* A play on the double sense of '*in grain*': (1) in corn; (2) dyed in grain; an ingrained knave.

IV. ii. 104. *Saved by the Helvetian translation.* I suppose this to mean Coverdale's Translation of the Bible; the first edition of which seems to have been printed at Zürich in 1535. See Preface to Coverdale's *Remains* (Parker Soc.), p. x.

IV. ii. 130. *Pared the devil's nails*: a stock incident in the Morality Plays. See the Clown's song in *Twelfth Night*, IV. ii.

IV. ii. 169. *Glories like glow-worms.* These lines occur again in *Vittoria Corombona*, p. 36 (Routledge's *Old Dramatists*).

IV. ii. 209. *The whistler shrill*: a common omen of ill. Dyce compares

> 'The whistler shrill, that whoso hears doth dy.'
>
> *Faerie Queene*, II. xii. 36.